BRAND TO THE BONE

GROWING SMALL BUSINESS INTO **BIG BRANDS**

BY
JACK SIMS

Brand to the Bone – Growing small businesses into Big Brands
By Jack Sims

Copyright © Jack Sims 2002

All rights reserved. No part of this book may be reproduced in any form or by any electronic or mechanical means, including information storage and retrieval systems, without written from the publisher, except by a reviewer who may quote brief passages in a review.

Published by: Palm Breeze Publishing
PO Box 694800
Miami
Florida.33269

Phone: 649 946 4136
brandtothebone@earthlink.com
www.jacksims.com

Cover design: Jim McNulty
Book layout: Jonathon Gullery
Printed in the United States of America
ISBN: 0.9725658-0-9

This book is dedicated to my amazing wife Kathi and my fantastic children, who have experienced the best and worst of me; I hope the best outweighs the bad.

"Once a customer has decided to buy the category and gets to the moment of truth, the point of purchase... If you have achieved a transfer of trust, a known and respected brand name turns the decision to buy your product or service into a shortcut."

Jack Sims

FROM THE AUTHOR

This is a book about starting and growing a business, but in particular, how to develop a brand, become a customer-focused organization thus enabling your company to grow and last you and your employees a lifetime. In my particular case, it was a marketing and promotion business, but the basics apply to any company, and I wish you all the success that I have enjoyed.

Over my 30 years in the marketing/promotion/advertising and brand-building businesses, I have learned from some really talented people and worked with some amazing clients who let us be as good as we could possibly be. Along the way I have made a lot of mistakes, as will you, but have also enjoyed some success. I created a company that stood for what I believed in, and I promoted the highest level of creativity and marketing sense.

There have been many lessons learned on the journey. These, together with many varied experiences, I am now going to pass along to you. Hopefully, they will collectively enable you to benefit and take the "safer route" to building a successful brand for your company, service, or product.

I would be remiss if I did not thank certain people who have helped me along the way on my incredible journey, which resulted in the best and largest marketing and promotion agency in the United States.

First of all, my father, for his amazing mind, business sense, and guidance, together with his assurance that he would always be there for me! My mother, for her belief that I should always reach for the stars! Jim McNulty, for his amazing ability to always have time to listen, and for being my best friend. Dick O'Brien, for never accepting creative mediocrity. Fran Grossman, who still doesn't believe she is the finest creative mind in the marketing/promotion business—Fran, you are! Ira Szot, thank you for being you! Karen Koslow, your ability to be decisive is infectious and your marketing thinking is unequaled. Larry

Swensen, there is only one greatest client, and you are it. Jack Daly, for giving me a new dream. Matt Savage, who just oozes taste and creative juices. T. Scott Gross for mentoring me in the speaking business and laughing along the way. And finally, Larry Bedosky, for having the ability to get it done. For every person I have been lucky enough to work with, you all know who you are, and you have my deepest thanks.

CONTENTS

Introduction: 11

Chapter 1:
Branding, the Concept:
The Durasol Awning Story..............................25

Chapter 2:
16 Steps to Launch a Brand............................35

Chapter 3:
Identifying Your Target Audience 67

Chapter 4:
Branding to the Bone....................................71

Chapter 5:
Total Branding—The 5 P's 85

Chapter 6:
16 Branding Musts..93

Chapter 7:
CRM: "It's the Customers, Stupid!"..................109

Chapter 8:
Think Like a Customer 127

Chapter 9:
Creating a Promotion
That Will Grow Your Brand!..........................133

Appendices:
Forms and Questionnaires............................141

INTRODUCTION

I believe in branding with a passion, a passion I hope I'll be able to instill in you so that you will be able to invoke it in your own company. If you follow some, if not all, of the suggestions that I make in this book, I assure you that they will make a difference in the long-term growth of your company—and in your company's bottom line. This then is the real meaning of brand equity, incremental company and shareholder value.

Let's play a little game. I want you to fill in the blanks:

Four words that tell you about a great household product: "Don't squeeze the _____."

Three words that tell you that you have just bought a great sporting goods product: "Just _____."

Two words that tell you the computer that you just bought is a great computer:
Because it has " _____."

And the one word that lets you know that these 3 products are leaders in their category is: "Brand."

There is so much awareness of these brands that everyone knows who they are—they are megaproducts, the leaders in their categories...they are **the brand leaders.**

What Is Branding?

There is no "definitive answer" to this question. It's like love: I know that I can define love in my mind, but it probably doesn't match your idea of what it is. You see, it's not like the legal or accounting businesses where there are generally accepted rules and standards to measure. Branding means different things to different people and there are no branding rules. In fact, there are more than one type of brand; for instance, I am at least 4 brands in my own life. I am "Honey" brand to my wife, "Dad" brand to my children, "Granddad" brand to my grandson, and also consultant/ author/speaker brand to my clients.

But in business, in its most simplistic form, branding consists of the following 4 points which form the outer part of my Branding Wheel concept. I cover this in chapter 5, the 5p's of Branding:

If you are a manufacturer of goods or deliver a service of any type, the one word that sums up branding is **PROMISE**. You make a branding promise to your customers to deliver products to an accepted standard and quality—all the product attributes, features and benefits and the many and various other claims that you communicate to the audience that is your customers. If you want to become a brand leader, keep your brand's promises.

If you are the recipient, the customer, the one thing that you have in your mind after receiving all of the information, advertising, communications, with the products features and benefits, is an EXPECTATION—a brand expectation. You have an expectation that the product or service will meet or even exceed the quality, value, standards, features, benefits, attributes of the product, or service that you intended to purchase.

The third part of the branding equation is that the brand is actually in the mind of the consumer: Brands are emotional, they are feelings—it's mental real estate that that the brand owns in the customers or prospects minds. These feelings can make the difference in the way your customers feel about your particular and your competition. So your objective is to get an emotional and creative connection with them and then a **BIGGER SHARE OF THEIR MIND** IN THE CATEGORY THAT YOU ARE COMPETING IN. I would like to give you an example of what I mean by "share of their mind." I am sure that you have all heard the expression "No one ever got fired for buying IBM." You'll notice that it doesn't say, "No one ever got fired for buying an IBM mainframe computer" or an "IBM laptop." You see, it's the assurance of the IBM brand that gives the confidence to the purchaser.

Which leads me to point #4, I assume that you are all in business to make money, because all of this branding and awareness is for you to get a **BIGGER SHARE OF THEIR WALLET** that they are spending in your category.

And that is what a successful brand is going to deliver for you, incremental profits and growing brand equity that equates to incremental shareholder value. Simply put: It increases profits as well as the value and sale price of your business!

UNDER YOUR SKIN

Recently I met an old friend I knew from the years I lived in St. Thomas, named David. When he was younger, David was a surfer, lived for the beach and the sun, had the usual branded look, long sun-bleached hair, baggy clothes, etc. I'd see him go through high school and then away to college in the States. During his college years he became a preppie. You know what that means, right? Head-to-toe Ralph Lauren! David had on a Ralph Lauren baseball cap, his polo shirt had the Polo logo on it, and his pants, socks, shoes, and belt all came from Ralph Lauren. He was a walking billboard for Polo clothes.

One day I was sitting on Sapphire Beach, watching a volleyball game when David turned up, dressed as usual in Ralph Lauren from top to bottom. They started to get into the game, and off came the logo'ed shoes and socks, then the baseball cap, then the Polo T-shirt. When he turned around, I realized that David was living vicariously through the Ralph Lauren brand. Tattooed on his left breast...yes, the Ralph Lauren Polo logo! After I stopped laughing, I realized the power of what I'd seen—

the power of what a brand image can get one of its customers to do. Of course, we can all imagine this is the kind of thing from a Harley-Davidson rider, but a Ralph Lauren preppie? I didn't think it was possible!

What does "brand to the bone" mean? It means that **your brand is not just the logo at the top of your letterhead or your packaging.** It's much deeper than that. It's the very essence of your brand. It's what your product stands for and the feeling it imparts to everyone in your company who touches the product. From the person who cleans the offices, to the president of the company, to the person who answers the phones, to the accounting department, the marketing department, shipping, manufacturing, research. All the steps in the sales chain, the guys on the shop floor, the guys who deliver for you…I don't care who they are: If they're involved with your product in some way, then they are involved in the branding process.

How does branding affect you? Well, it really doesn't matter what you do. I don't care if you're a plumber, an accountant, a TV repairman, or a major manufacturer. **You are part of a category and you do have a brand.** Whether you like it or not, every product that goes to market is part of a category. We call the products or services that are the biggest players in any category the "brand leaders." That's why it's so important to develop your brand strategy, implement it, and then become a brand leader.

On a practical level, here's how it works. You have been working all morning and decide that you have to get out of the office. You decide to go to the supermarket to buy a piece of fresh fruit. You go to the fruit and vegetable department and decide that you want an orange. You see 2 sections of oranges and pick up one from each section. You look at them both, feel and squeeze them (we all do it), and then realize that one of them has the Sunkist sticker on it! The question is, which one will you buy? Obviously, you'll buy the Sunkist orange. But the question is, Why? ***Because over the years Sunkist has delivered a great-looking, great-tasting orange. They are juicy, fresh, and the brand has become synonymous with great taste, an assurance that you will enjoy this orange.*** Sunkist meets or even exceeds the **PROMISE** it makes to its consumers, and that is why it is the brand leader in its category. That's branding in its most simplistic form. A good brand is the added value that comes into play at the moment of truth, which is the point of purchase—it turns the decision for consumers into a shortcut **(EXPECTATION AND BIGGER SHARE OF MIND).** I would also assert that if the Sunkist orange cost a penny or 2 more, then you would pay it **(BIGGER SHARE OF WALLET).** Now think about it: Isn't that how you want your customers to think about your product or service? Their decision is made easy, and they relate to your product enough to pay a premium price for it.

A taste of English branding!

I was born in England, but I am a naturalized American. Which leads me to a youthful memory that illustrates my second point about the way branding works inside your company.

I'm remembering a candy bar kids in the United Kingdom buy when they go to the beach, or "the seaside," as they say over there. The candy is called "a Stick of Rock." It's usually about a foot long and an inch or so in diameter. The outside is pink, and the inside is white and peppermint-flavored. What's so unique about this? If you look at the end of the stick, you see that it has the name of the town where it was bought "printed" on the end, and this name goes through the whole length of the rock—you see, the candy is extruded. So if you cut it up into pieces, suck on it, or chew on it, the name of the town is always readable.

This idea has dictated how I've worked with my clients and how I would like you to start looking at your brands. Your brand identity should go all the way through everything that your company touches—every piece of product, every person who works in the company, and right on down to the consumer and your suppliers. So try to think about the stick of Rock when you are reviewing the branding within your company. The brand should go all the way through every level of the product and every person in the company, it should be branded to the bone. Everyone who works with you, everyone who works for you, everyone they talk to: They represent the brand, they are the brand. *And if they don't understand that they have a significant impact on the brand, then it's your job to tell them. If they don't have the tools and the right instructions for branding, then they can't possibly get it right!*

Have you registered your brand or position statement?

Do you know how many brands are registered in the United States? I checked with various government offices to find out, but no one could give me a realistic answer. The only thing they would confirm is that there are millions and millions of brands on the market today. The best information that I could find indicates that there are about 3 million registered brands in the U.S. And those are only the registered ones! There will be 400,000 new brands registered in 2002 alone. (This doesn't sound like a lot, but we are not talking about registering a business, which everyone has to do.)

You don't have to register or trademark your brand, company, or positioning statement, but I would strongly suggest that if you are thinking about growing your company or product into a serious contender, then you should consider taking out this type of brand protection. For instance, after a seminar I gave in Florida, a president of a company came up to me and told me that they had received a letter from Mobil telling his company it had to cease and desist using the Pegasus logo on its stationary. Apparently, Mobil has the trademark on the Pegasus logo. The same happened at a diner that I sometimes eat at, where the owner asked for my help; apparently, he had also been given a cease-and-desist letter, this time from the Lexus car company. His diner was named "The Lexus Diner"; now he has to change it after 15 years of business. Probably the best-known case is the one involving Ralph Lauren: They own the word "Polo," so the United States Polo Association can't use it. So I urge you to make sure that you have the protection that you should have, especially if you are intending to get some serious growth for your company. There are lawyers who specialize in getting this done, and it really doesn't cost a lot; well worth it, in my opinion. (By the way, "Brand to the Bone" is protected—I do walk the walk!)

I do know that there are around 30,000 brands in the average supermarket. Wal-Mart has around 300,000 different products on its shelves. That's a lot of brands, and though yours may not be in the supermarket, you get the idea. There are a lot of brands out there. There are a lot of brands for you to compete against. *How are you going to get noticed?*

Well, that's what **BRAND TO THE BONE** is all about. I will give you some advice and branding insights that I believe will help you to walk away from this book with the tools that will enable you to make your brand into a brand leader. *This is the kind of knowledge that the major companies have and use. And I should know, because I've given this advice to some of those blue-chip clients myself.*

Branding is not only *achievable* by small companies without a lot of experience, it is *critical!*

Even if you are a two-person start-up, branding will work for you; it can be the major difference between you and your competition. In its purest terms, branding represents a transfer of trust between you and your customers, based on a perceived value and an expectation that you consistently live up to. No matter how small you may be now, successful branding will make you bigger. Many smaller companies think that branding is only for the national brands; in reality, the national brands have to advertise and promote as much as they do because they do not have what a small local company has. The local company has the ability to really understand what its customers want and has the opportunity to discuss those wants with them every day. If you are a local brand, stand tall: Your customers come to you for a real, valid reason—you deliver a product that they want and at a price that they think is value for the money. Just think about this: The reason that your local restaurant is still in business is because over time they have found out what you as a customer want, and they deliver personal service to you every time. This, despite the fact that national chains like Applebee's (your neighborhood restaurant), The Olive Garden, and T.G.I. Friday's are trying their very best to take all of their business away.

Think about the song from the TV show **Cheers**, "where everybody knows your name"—the local bar or pub gives you a comfort level that you just can't get in a national chain. That's why you go to your local bar or restaurant: Even though you can get the same beer, wine, or liquor anywhere, you still favor a certain bar or restaurant. The difference in national brands and local ones is the experience that you get when going through the purchasing cycle. The national brands put in programs to train their personnel to act like they are local, but that just doesn't always work. They usually work using the "Think nationally, act locally" concept. But how many times have you gone into a fast-food restaurant and been ignored by the young kids working behind the counter, or waited in line for much longer than you thought you should? Is the "fast food" that good; does it taste homemade? Local companies are the real deal: Just make sure that you provide the customers with great products that they want—great service that they can't get anywhere else—and the fear of low margins will start to fade. Many of the national brands have realized that the local store has a big advantage that they cannot compete with. Consequently, brands like Charles Schwab and Apple are beginning to open up stores on Main Street in an effort to get closer to the people in the neighborhood.

Why should you want to build your brand?

There are many reasons, and as you go through this book you will hopefully find reasons that are particularly pertinent to you and your brand. But probably the most relevant to you, if you are the owner or leader of a company, is the effect that it will have on your bottom line. You see, the difference that you should be looking for is the increase in owner or shareholder value and how your brand can make a positive impact on your bottom line. When I sold my second company, it was initially to an English firm, Boase Messimi Pollit, and it was during the period when the Brits were buying practically everything in the advertising and marketing business that was not nailed down. The interesting thing is how they were able to raise the money to buy the company: One of the big differences between U.K. and U.S. accounting systems is the way that they look at brand equity. In the U.K. brand equity is looked in a much more favorable light, and companies have even gone so far as to include it as an asset on their books, at least internally; for some reason, we don't do that yet in the States. This just doesn't make sense to me—it's like saying that the brand name "Coca-Cola" is worthless! The only time we in the U.S. actually address what brand equity might be is when we go to sell a company—then we call it "goodwill," which includes many things, such as ongoing sales and what the influence of the brand might be to the future of the business. I would like to suggest that you consider putting a number in your internal accounts under the "asset" column that reflects the value of the brand: the brand equity. This is a number that should be observed and monitored so that everyone in the company is made aware of it—in fact, brand equity could be used as one of the measurements for bonuses or paychecks.

"Branding," Warren Buffett once wrote in an annual report, "Brand is like a moat around your business." A strong brand can protect you against competitive attacks, market fluctuations, and price wars, and it can protect your premium price positioning. When all things are equal, consumers will buy the brand leader.

Do you have a Brand Commitment Statement?

Over the years I've worked with many major companies and with some incredibly talented people. We were very fortunate to have been successful; the company I started as a one-man band in 1976 became the largest marketing and promotion agency in the U.S. Just for the record, it wasn't always easy. I did slip and fall a few times. And just like you, on occasions I had to pay the staff without paying myself.

I am sure that one of the reasons we were successful is that everyone knew where I stood. I truly believe that great companies usually have great leaders who leave no doubt where they stand and empower their people to invoke their vision. All our clients and all the people who worked with me shared my vision. It was encapsulated in what I call the **"Brand Commitment Statement,"** and this is mine:

> "It is the work that counts—it's the work,
> it's always the work, and it's all driven toward
> making our clients more successful."

In everything you do, you have to make sure that everyone knows and shares your commitment to the brand. You also have to empower your employees to invoke your **"Brand Commitment Statement"**; it is one of the main ingredients in making your brand a brand leader. Once you have created and instituted your Brand Commitment Statement, you have to make sure that your fellow workers are empowered to enact it. Otherwise, frankly, it's just not worth the paper it's written on. You never want to have people in your organization say to a customer, "Oh, I have to ask someone about that, I'll get back to you."

Here is what they should ask themselves—this is from Rick Rose, and I believe it is probably the best empowerment action statement I have heard.

Is it right for the customer?
Is it right for the company?
Is it morally and ethically correct?
Is it something that you are willing to be accountable for?
Is it something that is generally in keeping with our best business practices?

If you can answer "yes" to all of these questions, don't ask, just do it!

Hire the right people, empower your people, and trust them and get them to think this way, and you will be on your way to making a difference and becoming a brand leader in your category.

If you don't have a **Brand Commitment Statement** then I urge you to get one. You can go online and check out companies like Johnson & Johnson or Dayton Hudson that have marvelous credos or mission statements. Use lines from mission statement books that are available online—I realize they are not your original words, and that's OK, as long as you mean the words in your heart. By the way, if you have a corporate mission statement, that's great, but your corporate mission statement is not your brand commitment statement. Your mission statement is the corporation's hopes, dreams, aspirations, etc. Your Brand Commitment Statement is specifically about what your brand will do or mean, to or for your customers. What you brand will stand for! It's the passion and the belief that counts! Having a Brand Commitment Statement is not the same as *living* a Brand Commitment Statement: Make sure you and your staff live it and that all of your customers are aware of what you stand for.

An example of the empowerment I am talking about occurred one day in our photographic studios: We were shooting something that involved models and food from our in-house kitchens, and this particular shoot was taking an inordinate amount of time. Now, if you have ever been on a shoot, you know it is always slow anyway, but this particular day, it was slower than normal. About 4 o'clock everyone was starting to get a little edgy, and the senior art director on the shoot started thinking that the shots would probably not get completed. She quietly checked to make sure that the studio was available the next day and that the models and the crew would be available too. At 6 p.m. she told the client that she was not going to get the shoot completed that day and had made arrangements to complete it the next morning. Well, you can imagine the client's reaction—this was going to cost a lot more, they had deadlines, etc. At 9:30 that night I got a call at home from the client, who started yelling at me about the costs and why didn't we get it done on time. After letting him get it off his chest, I quietly told him that the reason that he had us as his agency was because we will not let the work go out until it's right! As for the cost, we would bear any extra expenses, but it was more important to him as the client, and us as the agency, to put out only the best work we can into the market. He eventually understood—and, incidentally, agreed to pay the extra costs. The message is: Stick to your Brand Commitment Statement; don't make it something that you just have hanging in your reception area.

What Does It Come Down to?

Consistency and passion are the 2 things that can really make your brand soar. Are you driven by the belief that your brand should be #1 in its category? How much do you really want it to happen? Do you care passionately about the way your brand is nurtured, developed, and presented to your target audience? Do you care passionately about the impression you make on your target audience? **The more quality impressions you make and the more consistent they are, the better the overall impact will be.** Do you act as if every impression that your staff and your company make on a consumer is lasting?

I would like you to consider thinking a little differently; Don't just accept what is normal in your industry—shake it up! Think about the way the industry does it and then think how you can make it better—how you can improve what is done after considering the customer's point of view. For instance, as a customer in the furniture business, why does it take 3 months to get a couch? It doesn't make sense! If I want to buy a car, why does it take 6 weeks? If I have been flying on the red eye from L.A. to New York, why can't I check into a hotel before 4 o'clock in the afternoon? Why is it impossible to get a person from AT&T on the line to talk about my telephone bill? It seems to have plenty of people to call me when it wants me to buy or convert to its service!

CHAPTER 1

BRANDING, THE CONCEPT: THE DURASOL AWNING STORY

There are many differing views from many people on what branding is all about. I have put together a statement that I believe encapsulates the simplest way to think about branding:

> "Once a consumer has decided to buy the category and gets to the moment of truth—the point of purchase...if you have achieved a transfer of trust, a known and respected brand name turns the decision to buy your product or service into a shortcut."

Let's think about this for a moment. Consumers who actually buy from the category you are in had to decide, at some time, that they wanted to purchase the product or service. This is because they had seen the product, experienced it, been told about it, read about, or seen the product in some sort of communication medium. At that point, they decided that they would like the product in their lives. Now, unless the product is an "impulse purchase," like a pack of gum at the supermarket checkout, it usually takes a reasonable amount of time to get to the next stage—the moment of truth: the point of purchase. At this stage, if you have managed to get them to trust you before this point, or even during the purchasing period, by having an ongoing dialogue (maybe by media, or direct mail, or other promotional marketing activity), you will have earned their trust. They then will be able to make a decision to purchase your product over the competition easily; it becomes a shortcut!

I'd like to discuss a case history of one of the brands I helped develop. I have had a client called Durasol Awnings for the last few years, and the story of our work together will give you a good idea of how a brand can be impacted.

Durasol is a retractable-awning manufacturer; their products are purchased by users who want them primarily for their own homes. Durasol is based in upstate New York and, when I began looking at them in 1993, they had about $2.5 million in sales, mostly around New York state. I gave some seminars and tuition to their people and their dealers, and I noted the product and the category it was in, and it was evident to me that the category was going to be explosive. I thought that Durasol could become leaders if we had the right plan and brand strategy and executed it well. Subsequently, the Durasol Team has managed to grow the company from sales of about $2.5 million in 1993–1994 to sales of $30 million in 2002. That's compounded growth of around 35% annually.

If you speak to Lars Dupont, the president of Durasol, he'll tell you that marketing and branding are significant reasons for its growth and success. The product is in what we call a "me too" category. I would bet money that when we started, if I had put each of the top 8 manufacturers' awnings on 8 houses and you stood across the street to look at them, you couldn't tell the difference between any of them. The fabric pretty much all comes from the same supplier, the motors all come from the same manufacturer. Basically, the only difference in the 8 brands is the lateral arms, and consumers just don't see them unless you're underneath the awning. So it really is about developing a brand and a brand name, and a point of difference to set the Durasol brand apart that counts. This together with the marketing programs and customer service that support that brand is what makes the difference.

DURASOL Awnings®

While the Durasol brand is not as well known as Nike or Coca-Cola, within the motorized retractable-awning market it is the #1 brand. I'd like to show you how the brand has evolved and then describe all the communications strategies we developed to support it. We began with the knowledge that the product was produced as well as it could be, an essential ingredient of any branding strategy.

Where do you want to go?

The **first** thing we did was to ask the all-important question: Where do you want to go? Once we had decided on that—in this case, a marketing plan to take us to a premium position in the market, thus enabling Durasol to command a higher price point—then we were able to start putting the building blocks in place.

Second, we looked at the structure of the company. You see, if you increase your sales, the worst thing that can happen is that you can't get the product to the customer in the time frame and quality they expect: In other words, you have to be sure your structure can support growth in sales. In Durasol's case, we quickly realized that it needed some new equipment if it were to go into the sales growth mode we felt was possible.

Third, we needed to find out who the target audience was, so we looked at the customer base. We researched the market by speaking to customers who had purchased our product as well as potential customers who had recently shown interest. We also talked to people who had looked at the category and decided against purchasing. From the whole range of questions we put to them, we were able to identify our real customers and learned where to focus our efforts. Importantly, it was a very different group that we thought it was. **That's a reality check for all of you.** Durasol thought that its market was "young marrieds" with a couple of kids. In fact, it turned out that its average purchaser was much older, had no kids in the house, and paid cash or used credit cards, virtually no-one was paying over time. While we were doing this research, we also found out that we enjoyed a 99.5% consumer satisfaction rate. Here's a Jack Sims–ism for you: **Make sure that the target you're aiming at is the target that buys your product or service.** My experience with Durasol shows you quite clearly how much better your advertising and promotion dollars will be spent when you're armed with this knowledge. Make sure that you know who your real customer is; don't accept demographics without doing the research. You have got to go deeper! Like Durasol, you may be surprised to find who is actually buying your product. Find out who these customers are and what motivates them. It is often not who you think it is.

Once we had established who the customer was, we then focused all our energies into reaching that specific group. Imagine how much more effective our efforts became.

A shade more beautiful

We then developed a positioning statement—what I call the "essence" of the brand. Your positioning statement is the line that usually goes under or after your brand name and is something that we will go into later in the book. In Durasol's case, it was the copy line: "A SHADE MORE BEAUTIFUL." All of the communication pieces and graphics were created to impart the impression of bringing the freshness of outdoors under a retractable awning. The overall look was to be somewhat aspirational, with clean lines and an uncluttered look and appeal to the target audience that we had identified.

One of the biggest factors in taking the business forward was our intention to create category awareness. We felt then, and still do today, that the awning category is still in its infancy in the U.S. The more we could gain category awareness and increase our brand share, the faster we would be on our way to becoming the brand leader in a growing market.

We hoped that if we could get customers' attention, we could create a need for an awning, then persuade them they'd be better off with a Durasol awning. You've all heard sales guys talk about "sticker shock." Well, what we found out was that despite what our sales guys were saying, price was not a major problem. Most of our purchases were made in cash or credit card; virtually no one asked to pay over time. Since the category was in its infancy, we knew that by stepping up to the plate and investing in really good corporate branding and marketing programs, we could grow our brand awareness and more than our fair share of the market.

We initiated an aggressive campaign that consisted of black-and-white and color print advertising, literature, POS (point of sale) materials, marketing books, public relations campaigns, and direct-mail programs that went out 4 times a year. Our continuing research revealed that the time between wanting to buy an awning and actually ordering one could take up to 18 months. So we kept on mailing until the consumer either bought or told us to stop; you have to make sure that you have an ongoing relationship with the prospective customer if you are going to earn their trust. In addition, we also developed a successful Web site that now gets over 30,000 hits per week. Finally, we produced a TV commercial that really shows the product to its maximum effect, and it gets shown in more markets as the sales area becomes nationalized. As you can see, all of the pieces in our plan look like they come from the same family—they are consistent in their message—and they have substantially helped grow the business.

Increase your living space... with the touch of a button!

Durasol Retractable Awnings offer you:

- *Instant, on-demand solar protection*
- *Reduced energy costs*
- *Added living space*
- *Touch-of-a-button operation*
- *Self-storing and maintenance-free convenience*

Durasol Retractable Awnings are designed to create a cool and natural extension to your home. They provide instant UV protection and conserve energy by lowering indoor temperatures by up to 20 degrees. Every awning is custom-made and professionally installed, so you'll be able to choose from a variety of colors and styles to suit your needs and fit your lifestyle. Call today, and experience a whole new way to enjoy outdoor living...at home!

DURASOL Awnings
A Shade More Beautiful.

Call toll free 1-877-123-4567, or visit us on the web at www.durasol.com

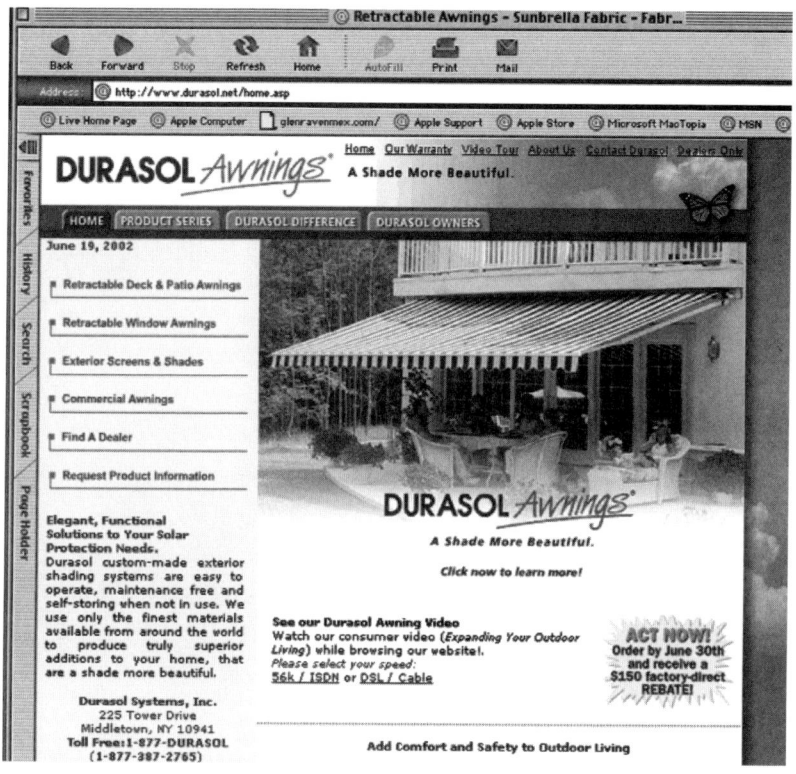

The management of Durasol was gutsy to go with our recommendations. As a result, we grew the awning market, grew Durasol's share of the awning market, and took Durasol from just the name of a company to a brand that stands for the #1 motorized retractable-awning manufacturer in the country. Consumers in the market for awnings will always research Durasol; it will always be considered for purchase. That's what branding can do. Durasol's management and its thinking about maintaining its "customers first" focus, together with the will to keep the energy level and the advertising communications up to the high standard it's set, will keep it #1 in its category for years to come.

CHAPTER 2

16 STEPS TO LAUNCH A BRAND

Over the years, mostly through trial and error, I have established the following 16 steps that I would recommend that you go through when you are about to launch or even relaunch your brand or company.

1. Develop a plan and goal for the company and for each product.

This is the exciting part: It really is the time when you are making decisions that could take your company and the people around you on the path to success. The goals should be lofty—"Reach for the stars," as my mother used to tell me. **Be a dreamer;** really dream of the success that would be beyond what you can normally think of. Why? Because every person I have ever met, who has started a successful business or had a great career, has been a dreamer. If you can't dream it, you can't do it! So make sure that you put down in writing what your hopes and dreams are for your business and make them as high as you can imagine. The actual planning process is something that will vary by person and company. However, there are many ways you can get the formula for developing a business plan; they are available on the Web at sites like Businesstown.com and others, as well as in special marketing and planning programs you can install that are available in most computer stores.

There are varying schools of thoughts regarding planning, and some will tell you that making a five-year plan doesn't make any sense at all. They say that if anyone can forecast the price of oil or the interest rates 5 years from now, then they are probably using a Ouija board. Because none of our most respected economists have ever been able to prophesy the price of raw materials, cost of labor, the stock market, or virtually any other criterion you can think of 5 years out! However, I think the opposite way: If you don't have a plan, if you don't know where you want to get to, then you can't possibly get there. And let's face it: If you fall short of a really lofty goal, you are still probably further ahead than you would have been if you did not have the goal in the first place.

I like to think of planning as like captaining a plane. If you captain a plane, you have to go through various checks before you can take off. First, you decide where you want to go! Then you get out your charts and start plotting a course that will get you there. It doesn't always go in a straight line; you pass over certain checkpoints so that you can confirm you are in the right place at the right time. You then work out the flying time, allowing enough fuel to get you there with at least 20% to spare, just in case. Then you check that the plane is in condition to fly. The final thing is to post the flight plan with the tower and get its permission to leave the airport and take off.

A business plan is just like this. You have to know where you want to get as well, putting the checkpoints along the way to make sure that you are on track. If you decide that you want to develop a five-year plan, know that you have to monitor it regularly. A five-year plan today soon only has 4 years, then three, then two…

Some of the questions that you might want to ask yourself as starters are:.

Why are you in business in the first place?

What type of business do you want?

What is the method of distribution?

Is your product used in conjunction with other products?

How healthy is the market that you are competing in?

Do you have the management and sales expertise to achieve the plan?

2. Decide on the product category you want to compete in.

While this sounds really basic, you really do have to think very carefully about this. Is the product or service you are in, or going into, relevant? Is the category current—is it what people want today but may not want tomorrow? One of my old clients, Polaroid, is a prime example of not being current, because the Polaroid camera is a product that is out-of-date. Consumers can get instant imaging through their digital cameras, no film required, and see everything on their computer or TV instantly! The same thing happened in the past to complete industries, like the pony express: Once the railroads came along, the pony express was obsolete. Like the steel industry, when other substances and forms of manufacture came along or the product was produced cheaper or more efficiently in another part of the world. Is the audience that will be buying your product literally dying off? Is it being replaced by the next generation, or do people simply not want your product? Every category has a sales curve, and eventually the curve will start to bend downward—just make sure that the category you are in is on the upswing! If you don't, then you will soon have to start competing on price; as the category becomes smaller, customers start looking for the cheapest price, and that's just not a place you want to be. So I would ask the following questions:

Why am I producing this product? Is it just something I know, or is it something that I know customers will want, and want for a long time?

What will make our product or service different from the competition? Why will consumers come to us?

How will we price our product in the marketplace? Do we

want to be a price brand or image brand? Just for the record, it's a lot easier to compete and win in the quality arena than it is in the price marketplace.

Is our product or service reliant on any other product or marketing factors that can affect the ability to go to market?

3. Produce a product that will compete with, and beat, the market.

Product quality—or, even better—*perceived quality*—is what I believe you should pay close attention to. The primary reason is financial: You really do not want to compete on price—someone, somewhere, can always beat you. Every category has a range of pricing that is acceptable, and I would strongly recommend that you position yourself at the top part of that range. By the way, customers usually value what they get in strict proportion to what they pay for it.

Perception is reality, the saying goes, and that is particularly true when it comes to marketing a product. For instance, the sneaker market has a 12-year-old boy or girl willing to pay $150 or more for a pair of sneakers because Michael Jordan says so! The inference is that they will make the wearer jump higher. Well, I recently did a test; being a runner, I have several pairs of sneakers in the house. I put 4 pairs on the floor and yelled at them, "Jump!" Not one pair even moved—amazing how that works!

As part of your overall product development process, you might want to ask yourself:

What are the 3 most compelling reasons that consumers will want to buy my product or service over the rest of my category's participants?

Why did I decide to produce this particular product? Why do I think customers will want to buy my particular brand of product versus the competition's?

What makes my product different—what is the USP (unique selling proposition)?

    Product quality can be measured in many differing ways: from the materials used; the design that you create; the service that you give; the level of satisfaction that meets or exceeds the customers' expectations. I would strongly suggest that you make the best possible product or service that you can—it's so much easier to sell a quality product, and to sell it for the long term. I believe product design can give you a significant opportunity to differentiate yourself from your competition. In the U.S. we tend to think more of the functionality of the product, as opposed to our European counterparts, who think of not only the practicality but also of the aesthetics and how the product or service might visually fit into their homes or lives. When I say "product," I do not only mean items that are physically produced or manufactured; I mean your products, goods, or services—yes, even if you are in a service industry you are still a product. Just because it's a commodity item or product, that does not mean it should not be pleasing to the eye. Try to make sure that you spend enough time creating whatever you bring to market to be as attractive as possible—people will always tend to buy or consider buying a brand that simply looks better. Remember, most of the consumer products are selected for purchase from an arena where there is no person aiding the sale. The product itself and the packaging (if any) have to look good; you have to reach the consumer at many levels, but a combination of product looks and an "emotional buy-in" are essential to get the approval to purchase. This can also be the reception area in your offices. Yes, that is still your product: It's like a great big billboard that advertises your product. Make sure it gives the best impression to visitors that it can, get it visited occasionally by someone who has never seen it before, and ask them to grade it on a 1 to 10, specifically spelling out what is wrong. They will be able to see it with an unjaundiced eye!

4. Determine who your real customers are.

The first thing that you have to do is determine is if there are any changes going on in the overall market that might affect the way your potential customers are going to think about your product. Are there different groups of customers for your product, and what makes them want or need to buy something from your product category?

Then you have to conduct research into the market to discover who your ideal target customer is. The size of your company and the geographic area in which you are selling will determine the quantity and the depth of your research. Most of us operate on the concept that we know the demographics of the people purchasing within the category. But I simply do not accept that—I believe that the status quo is not acceptable. The best way to find out who your ideal customers are is by going out and asking them!

For instance, let's say the normal demographics might suggest that your category is bought by women ages 25–55, college-educated, income of $80,000, married with 1.2 children in the home. That's just not good enough: Can you imagine why a 25-year-old woman is compared to a 55-year-old? You need to get closer—find out who the real decision-makers are and what they are doing 24-7, a week in the life of that person. Basically, find out what that person does all day, every day, for a week, to the best of your capability. Then put together a mental or even a visual replica of what the target might look like and give the person a name. This is what we did for a consulting client of mine; we named the fictional character "Mildred." Then every time we were working through a problem relating to the brand—what advertising to use, what packaging will have the most impact, etc.—we simply had to ask ourselves, "What would Mildred think about this? What would her reaction be?"

There are also standard operating procedures that you should consider using—things like focus groups or mall intercepts that are normal ways to get to talk to your target audience, and these certainly should become part of your arsenal. Some of the things that you should consider asking your potential customers are: What are the factors that might inhibit their spending in the category? What are their lifestyles? Who actually makes the final decision to purchase?

5. Decide who will take responsibility for the brand.
This is probably one of the most important parts of developing a brand-leading product or service. You must have one person who takes full responsibility for the brand. In major packaged-goods companies there are brand managers, and it doesn't matter how small your company is, you need that person too! It might well be you if you are the head or owner of the company, and I am absolutely certain that no one is capable of looking after your company the way you can; you should really be the person who drives it. You have to be the most enthusiastic person on the brand team—your enthusiasm should be pervasive throughout your company, and you should be the champion. You may well be a big enough company to have a marketing department, but even so, I would still strongly recommend that you should be the driver of the company or brand marketing. Your passion for your brand has to trickle down!

**6. Create the brand name, graphic image,
positioning statement (or tag line), and trademarks.**
This part of the development of your branding will probably require you to seek some outside help; it's also the one area that you should spend some money on. Remember, whatever brand name, image, or positioning you create will be seen by your target audience on a regular basis. The amount of money spent should be very carefully thought through, because you will be putting a lot more money behind bringing these impressions to the notice of your target audience. The net result will be that you'll get a tremendous amount of impressions from this creative

production, so try to think of it as paying per single use of it, and then the amount you pay to develop your creative impression becomes a minuscule amount.

Creating a brand name is oftentimes attempted by people who, in all honesty, have no formal creative training to do so but are directly involved with the company. That doesn't mean that you can't do it—simply that it really does take a person or group of people who do have formal training or a great deal of experience at doing this sort of thing. However, before you start any of the creative processes, I would strongly advise you to create a brief that you will want answered by the creative group. Frequently, the agency or creative folks will put the brief together for you, and I do not think that's the right thing to do. You are in charge of your company—you are, in theory (and, I hope, in practice), the marketing director. The request and guidance for any of the creative services should come from you, and all presentations of work should be measured against this creative brief.

The use of the creative briefing form gives all parties involved in the process the chance to be measured against the factual information available and the required direction that you want the particular project to go. (A sample creative briefing form is in the appendix.)

This part of the brand communication system development is what we refer to as "corporate identity," and there are many companies that specialize in just this alone. I would strongly suggest that, if you can afford it, you use one of these expert companies, especially if you are really serious about becoming a brand leader in your category. However, if you want to create your own, I suggest that you do it in 3 steps: first, the brand name; then, the logo; and finally, the positioning statement.

Start with the actual brand name: Think about those who are the target audience and what it is looking for in your category vis-à-vis what the brand promises to deliver. What will be the feeling when they use the product or service? What feeling can they expect when using the product? The category that you are in may well dictate the direction you have to take. But the words have to deliver a memorable communication that delivers on the emotional wants, needs, hopes, aspirations, or confidence that customers are looking to get from the brand. In actual fact, the brand name often does not mean anything to start with—it takes time, and consistent, numerous quality impressions, to create a successful brand name and position.

For instance, we all know the "Swoosh" logo that Nike uses as its "thumbprint," or image. They have Tiger Woods, Michael Jordan, and dozens of other famous sportsmen and women wearing the "Swoosh" on their clothing. Nike has spent millions of dollars ensuring that it gets consistent impressions anytime the logo is used. But it's a well-known story: A young female design student from Portland, Oregon, designed the Nike logo. Nike paid approximately $85 for the design, and frankly, it's a good design. But it would mean nothing if Nike had not managed to build a brand behind the logo and use multiple quality impressions to support it.

A positioning statement is something that supports and reinforces the positioning that you are trying to own in the customer's mind. Ideally, it should be a statement you can say about your product or service that your competitors cannot. If that is not possible, then when you have developed the positioning statement that you want to use in support of your logo, then please make sure that you trademark it. It's just like taking an insurance policy out: You don't want to be using something for years only to find out that someone else owns it and you have to start all over again. The third step is the logo, though sometimes you do not need one at all—with my Durasol Awnings client, its name is the logo, and a logo is definitely the thumbprint that holds all of the communications together. This will take the service of a good creative group, and you must make sure that you test your customers' reactions to the logo. You don't have to like it, but your customers do! Your logo is going to be with you for a long time, and it's going to be seen—hopefully, huge amounts of people, many times—so find the right people to create it and make sure your customers like and understand its relevance.

Develop the brand strategy, objectives, and positioning.
Hopefully, you will gather throughout this book that your customer is the single most important person in your company—the customer buys your brand! Therefore, your brand strategy has to start with your customer; it's what he or she thinks and feels, not what *you* or your marketing team think. To be successful in the future, you have to become a brand-focused and customer-centric company. You probably have a company organizational chart, and like most organizational charts the president or CEO is in the top box. I would like you to add another box on top, and put **customer** in that box: Customers are the most important components of your company.

I have found over the years that most of the work you have to do in bringing a product to market or improving a brand's growth is usually common sense. Like developing a brand strategy, one can only start at the beginning. The beginning is to establish the brand (or, of course, where the brand is right now) in the eyes of your current customers.

In developing the brand strategy, you have to clearly identify where you are going. If you don't know, you just can't get there! When you develop your strategy, please try to remember the KISS concept: "Keep it simple, silly."

Once you have established where you want to go, you have to confirm exactly where you currently are as a brand, the category, your customers, competition, and what the economic climate and indicators are. You need to know things like:

The category trend: Is it in a growth, stable, or declining

stage? (You can probably get some good information on market trends from trade magazines or associations.)

What is the expected value of the category, and what sort of share of that market can you realistically be likely to get over the next 5 years?

What are the key points that decide the marketplace: product features? Lifestyle usage of the product? Is the product currently a regional brand that has national potential? Is it a year-round product or limited by seasons?

How many players are in the category—what are their individual shares of that market, and what is the condition of each of these competitors, to your best guess?

You also have to determine how your competitors are going to market: What methods and vehicles are they using to reach their customers? What is their strategy—how are they positioning themselves in the market, and can you (or do you want to) compete against their position? Maybe you would like to create a new position that fulfills a current untapped need or want.

Complete an in-depth analysis of their company, which might include quality, sales force, advertising, number of employees, strengths and weaknesses, etc., and rank them on a scale from 1 to 10 in each category. Do the same for your company to see how you compare.

After analysis, you need to decide how many differing groups of potential customers are there for the product or service you are going to supply. What is the range of pricing that is acceptable in the category, and where do you want to be in it? I will tell you that being the **low-cost producer** is great, but don't be the **low-cost provider:** You can always be beaten on price, and again, that just isn't a place you want to be. Find out what the experts in the industry are forecasting for changes in the product; decide what impact such changes will have to the way you launch or grow your brand. Try to estimate what the size of the market will be for the next 5 years, based on all of the information you can get; are there likely to be any dramatic movements in the selling price of your product or service?

DO YOU HAVE A POINT OF DIFFERENCE?

Now is the time to find out if you have a POD (point of difference) between you and your competitors: Does it have a technical edge? Is it more reliable? Does it perform quicker or have some other major benefit? You also have to be really honest with yourself—admit what weaknesses you might have and decide how you might be able to overcome them.

You should then be able to decide what is the upside potential for the brand, and therefore be in a good position to start establishing a launch or relaunch plan. You can't have enough information, especially regarding who your potential customer is, and I cover this in the next chapter.

After you gather all of this information, you will be at the point where you can start to find out what is the "essence" of your brand: What is its heart and soul, as well as its practical applications and uses? There are many attributes that can be used to promote the essence of the brand, and it's your job to find out what the most appropriate and effective one might be for yours. It might be a sensory advantage: Cinnabon makes sure that wherever its stores are, the fabulous aroma that comes from its products permeates the area around the store. It could be a message like Weight Watchers' which is basically "We will make you slimmer." It could be the safety message that Volvo uses in all of its car advertising. A message or position calling attention to the product's status as an import usually fetches a premium price: Häagen-Dazs ice cream has done this successfully (although, of course, it is an American-made product). It could be a service-and-speed message like Jiffy Lube's. Other messages could be the actual design; that the product has a 100% guarantee; that the product is fun; that you'll get instant gratification, like from a truffle; and on and on.

The key thing is that you should be consistent with your position—it takes a long time to get the consumers to associate your brand with your particular essence or product advantage, so stick with it if your research shows that it's the way to go. You know the category that you are in, but the important thing is, what makes you different—why would your target audience choose you over your competitors?

You have to make sure that you find your own competitive advantage; what is your "mousetrap," and how can you improve it? One thing that will help you become the leader in your category is by acting like a leader: Offer your company, product, or service to the trade and to media, letting them know that you are experts in the category and are available for comments or opinions. You somehow have to find something that will separate you from the pack—the industry calls it a USP (unique selling proposition)—and once you find it, stick with it. I have seen it happen so often: People change their strategy without really giving it a chance to work.

Decide on the mood, tone, and image that you want the brand to have.
This part of the business is incredibly difficult to cover, particularly if you have not had any creative training or experience. Unfortunately, we all think that we are capable of being creative directors, and without experience, we become our own worst enemy. I can't tell you how many times I have shown creative work to clients who decided on the imagery by debating it with their secretary or their spouses. (By the way, if you are in business at all, you do have an image with your customers, albeit embryonic if you are just starting out.) The thing is that you may have low brand awareness and your image may be somewhat unknown. But if your image is not as good as it should be, you can put a plan in place to change it. It's much easier to change your image when your brand is still small.

But I would make sure that you decide the mood, tone, and imagery that you want the brand to have is easily and eagerly associated by the target audience. The direction should be written in your creative brief, where you decide whether you are positioning the brand as a premium, average, or low-priced product. Then you are in a position to decide what the key visual communication elements are that will support that position. For instance, the Durasol brand has a very "all-American" red, white, and blue logo that is easily read. The way the "Awnings" part is illustrated clearly indicates that this is a fun product. The positioning statement "A shade more beautiful" communicates the use of the product, since research has shown that one of the primary features and benefits from the product that consumers want is "shade." It also demonstrates that the Durasol Awning that they have installed on their home will beautify it. The overall mood and tone is clean-cut and aspirational in manner. The tasteful graphics show the product itself, the awning, as the main feature. Because the category is in its infancy and we needed to get awareness, even if it benefited our competitors, the actual brand name was subservient to the awning; this, however, will change gradually as the awning market starts to mature. Also, the homes and awnings that were featured in the advertisements were changed to correspond to the areas of the country that were being targeted in the advertising. People in the Northeast have wooden decks on the backs of their homes, while homes in the West have patios—so generally, the look is dramatically different. Therefore, we changed the look of the homes so the audience in each market would be comforted by seeing homes that are typical in its area, thus enabling them to make a personal connection with the brand.

9. Conduct research to ensure that the creative approach achieves the image with the target audience.
One of the biggest reasons for conducting research is that, to be truthful, **our** opinions don't really matter that much. We are so close to the product or service we are trying to market that

our opinions are probably tainted anyway. This does not mean to say that you should not involve people in the company to evaluate the new advertising campaign—you should, and for various reasons. First of all, the fact that you are actually asking for their input tells them that they are valued and appreciated in the company; believe me when I tell you that this will do wonders for morale. I mentioned earlier that your customers are the best barometers you can get for analyzing any of the creative programs that you want to bring to market, and that is true. In my experience, research takes various forms: There is the basic inside-the-office focus groups; people that know and have bought your product or category; and of course, the people who have not bought the category at all. In addition, there are now online groups that can give virtually instant feedback to any type of question or creative program that needs evaluating. You can use a company to arrange and hold the focus groups, or it is possible to do it yourself. However, if you do want to conduct your own research, please make sure that you put the appropriate amount of time in preparation for these groups. There are several things that you will have to do to make it happen.

First, you have to know why you are doing it: What are you expecting to get out of the research? What decisions will it enable you to make? Then, you need to prepare the questions that you really want answered; these, of course, will vary by the type of research you are doing. Next is making arrangements to gather the research focus group attendees; they will be a lot easier to find if you are using a research company—that's its job. Otherwise, you will have to get your sales staff, or any member of your staff, to find people who are potential members of the focus group. The event normally is conducted at premises that are designed specifically for them. The meeting is conducted by a trained facilitator who addresses the group, asks the questions, and leads them where you want them to go—all behind a 2-way mirror so that you can see the body language and hear the answers to the questions. The key thing is, if you are proposing an advertising campaign that is incorporating or using your logo, positioning statement, mood and tone, visual communication, promotional programs, and so forth, you need to make sure that you get input on every single area— because those in the focus group are the types of people who will buy the product or service. What do they feel about it? What emotion do they get when looking at it? Will they buy or probably buy it? Is it believable? Do you trust the provider? Cover as many areas as you would like. But in conclusion, I would suggest that you use a research company as soon as your growth allows for it.

10. Develop a marketing plan that will achieve the brand objectives.

The following is an outline of the thought process as well as steps that I suggest you go through in developing a marketing and/or business plan. There are volumes of books and articles that try to articulate specific and scientific guidelines, but after 25-plus years of marketing experience and personal involvement in many product launches (some successful and some not), the following is my process:

Start with the idea. Typically, a product concept, product, or service. Think of it just sitting there with no place to go. Will the idea be attractive to the people who would actually pay good money for it (i.e., the target audience)? Sure, you can develop a marketing plan on anything. But the ones that are done on products or services that are not close to your heart and the potential customer's heart are plans that are typically done with smoke and mirrors, because you just don't know, and are hard-pressed to find out, what the real motivation is.

Get to know the product: Touch it, feel it, get to know the emotion that you feel when you use the product or service; get to know any strengths or weaknesses. Take the product with you, if it is small enough; put it somewhere that you can constantly see it. Ask your friends, kids, and other family members about it: what they like, what they don't like, and most importantly, would they buy it and for how much. Listen to what they say. You need to be really honest here—don't fall prey to shortcuts or bias. Make sure that you spend enough time with the product to ensure that you really know it and get some sort of emotional attachment that can be qualified. I suggest that you try the product out for yourself repeatedly and fully understand what you are asking others to invest in. Also, try to avoid the euphoria of get-rich-quick schemes; they usually fizzle out quickly.

Now that you have a really good feel for the product or service, begin to craft a **Vision Statement** for the business. What are your goals? Be specific. Do you want to create a category? Gain a specific share of an existing category? Be a fast follower or a first mover? Make the Vision Statement the first page in your marketing plan. Be concise, specific, and make it measurable and time-bound.

Next, look around. See who else is offering the product or service. Check out the competition and start to track product comparisons, pricing, merchandising, communications, and any other data you can collect. This is called **Competitive Analysis,** which is one component in establishing a **Current Condition** of the market. In addition to competitive products, take the time to understand the industry as a whole, including trends, issues, pending technology developments, and other opportunities, risks, and threats—it is really the first chance for you to understand where you stand and the work ahead of you. This could also be your first opportunity to make major course corrections, including recommending termination or cancellation of the program.

Talk to as many people as you can—consumers, retailers, analysts, and manufacturers—and listen to what they say. I use the assumption that people are typically honest; if what you hear conflicts with what you think, circle back and reevaluate your original thinking. Be realistic—expect the worst but hope for the best.

Take the first step: Start to craft the plan. What are the benefits of your product or service, and who is the target market? And how do you expect to articulate those values to the shopper or end user if you have a product that is in a 2-step distribution category? What do you have, and why will people want to buy it? Take the time to document the key strengths of your proposition; these will become the foundation of your plan and are what will become your **Business Strategy.** You are in a war to capture a bigger share of the consumers' wallets, and you are one in a thousand marketers lobbying for the cash. What's your story? What can you say that will catch the consumers' attention?

Determine the real size of the market. Truly understand the lay of the land, and be honest. You need to think about the real size of the category, how relevant your product or service is to the target market, and then anticipate that most of your target market really has other priorities. This is called **Market Analysis,** and careful research and understanding of the market will be key in setting and achieving a realistic plan. Under-promise and over-deliver — every time!

If you are convinced that an opportunity exists, do the details. Write an outline of your business plan.

a) What is the business concept?

b) What are the assumptions used in your business plan?
c) Objective of the business

d) Organizational objectives
      1) Outline of business team and roles
      2) Candidates to fill the positions
      3) Be realistic!

e) Outline the Current Condition

1) Market size and growth projections: Identify the target market; County, State, Region, U.S., North America, The Americas, Europe, Asia, or Worldwide? How big is the market for your product? How many likely users/purchasers of your product exist, and what is the likelihood that they will use/purchase your product, identify them by region or target market. Should the total be discounted—how much advertising or merchandising support will be required by market? Take the total available market, then discount or adjust for outside influences.

2) Who are the players in the category, what is their competency? Who are the other manufacturers that have products in the category? What are their products? How capable are those manufacturers in commercializing their product in your markets? Do they have a demonstrated history of commercializing products or services? Are they good or bad…what are their strengths and weaknesses?

3) Photos of products, services, and merchandising, as well as product samples.

f) Target market

1) Who will buy the product, and why?
2) What are the buyers' choices, and why will they choose you?

g) Product or service strategy

1) Current offering: Current versus going forward—if you only plan to have a single offering (not always a good thing for the long haul), then you should do the aforementioned exercise against products in the market only. However, you should anticipate the competition's strategic plans and direction and analyze your future offerings (or vision) against what you expect from the competition. The competition will possibly introduce a new product in the next 6 months, in 12 months, and then 18 months. Companies do not typically introduce a single prod-

uct; anticipation of their next move could be your strategic advantage. Retailers and customers like to know that there is a plan and a step-up strategy.
    2) Show that you are committed and will be around.

h) Operations
    1) Who will manufacture your product, and where?
    2) Who will handle service and returns?

I) What resources will be required to provide the product or service?
    1) Packaging strategy
    2) Branding strategy
    3) Positioning
    4) Communications
    5) Merchandising
        a) Strategy
        b) Implementation plan

j) Promotions strategy

k) Partnership strategy

l) Sales strategy

m) Retail
    Strategy: Are you targeting specific channels or retail accounts? (Is your business built on a mass-market retail distribution plan, or does it involve electronic stores?) Is the plan built on a slow rollout or a major blitz for your introduction? In either case, what are your assumptions?

    1) Timing: When do you expect to be in retail? In how many accounts?

    2) On how many counters? When? Literally calculate by month by retailer.

3) Account build: This is a bottom-up calculation of the number of retail accounts that will sell your product. How many actual stores within a retail chain will participate, and when? Literally list the account name and number of stores (counters) involved over a given period of time—e.g., 6 months, 12 months, and beyond.
4) Retail pricing and margins
5) Retail development strategy

n) Cost of sales assumptions:
What are the assumptions used in the business plan?
Outline the specifics that you have assumed in creating your business plans—the strengths and weaknesses of your plan.

Objectives of the business?
What are your real goals of the business—you are probably not doing it because you love to work. What are your financial goals for the business? What are your strategic goals for the business? (Do you want to create a new category? Do you want to become the leader in a category? Do you want to displace competition in the category? Quantify.)

Organizational objectives
Outline of business team and roles. What resources do you need? Why? What are their skill sets? What will they be expected to do? What is the reporting responsibility?

Candidates for the positions!
Who are the people you have in mind for the positions? Where are they now, and will they move to your company?
Be realistic!

Don't overshoot your goals by listing every possible position in the world. But on the other hand, don't build a business plan with you as the boss, chief cook, and bottle washer.

o) Financials
    1) Profit and loss
    2) Balance sheet
    3) Monthly sales forecast
    4) Monthly retail account build
    5) Expenses
    a) Sales
    b) Marketing
    c) Administration
    d) Finance
    p) Ratios and analysis for bankers or investors
    q) Milestones
    r) Concerns and issues

Got the plan done? Pass it around and **get some other opinions.** Refine, adjust, and of course, correct if necessary. A plan is just the starting point and should be viewed as a working document. It will probably be wrong or incomplete the first few times you work with it. But if you make the adjustments and continue to refine it regularly, you will end up with a document that will live with you for a really long time—one that you might actually use to run the business!

11. Decide on outside sources for advertising, promotion, public relations, packaging, product design, direct agencies—then make sure they are all team players, clearly understanding that the brand must be the star!

When you are large enough to have a support team able to help you to take your products to market, there are some very basic things that you should remember. Make sure that you look at several companies to make sure the fit is right. A relationship with any agency is like a marriage: You both have to want the relationship to succeed, and there will be times when things don't always go the way everyone intends them to. But the most essential part is to make sure that both companies are on the same wavelength, both emotionally and in the vision that you have for the growth of your brand. Check to make sure that the agency has a good working knowledge of the business you are in. It need not have had experience in your specific product or service, but it should have some experience in the category or a similar one.

The first step is to make sure that the chemistry between the companies is on track; have a sense of humor because, believe me, there will be times when both companies will need one. Naturally, the agency has to run a reliable shop, and you must feel comfortable that it will always tell you the truth. You must feel confident it is making a profit on your account, but at the same time, have a comfort level in knowing that you are getting value for the money.

As I have said, you must try to run a customer-centric company, and any agency has to be in absolute agreement with this. I can't tell you how many times I have seen agencies dictate the route that the campaign should go, often to the detriment of the brand. The relationship has to be a win-win for both companies, and keep in mind that the ideas can come from anywhere—there are no bad ideas, only ones not said.

In terms of creativity, an agency has to be able to bring a style that your brand is looking for, and the agency should present itself in a manner that will encourage you to put it in front of your customers.

Make sure that it has the primary talent in-house; so often, agencies are actually using freelance talent to try to win your account. Check that the talent pitching for your account will be working on it if they get it.

Find out if the agency works on the normal 17.65% markup on all outside purchases, including media. Find out if this is in fact the best way for the parties to work together. I have seen companies bill everything at cost and charge an overall fee for their work. There are no cemented methods anymore; I have even seen an agency prepare to work on the assumption that if it gets significant gains in sales it will share in the profitability, which could well exceed its normal fee. But this, of course, will be earned only if it exceeds the agreed sales numbers; this really makes the agency aware that it will only be rewarded for one thing—making the sales needle move.

Naturally, the agency you choose will have to have all of the normal capabilities, like creative design, copy development, and a good working knowledge of all of the various disciplines: advertising, promotions, marketing, direct response, Internet, bill board, media placement, planning, TV and radio airtime purchasing. There are many other areas that you might need to get your agency involved in, so make sure that it has the expertise to work on, or can get produced, packaging, point-of-purchase materials, and—especially—knowledge of the arena that your product actually sells in. For instance, if your product sells through retail outlets, a strong working knowledge of that type of channel is essential: There are so many mistakes that can be made—you don't want to be teaching your agency how to get the product to market, on your dime.

Check if that the agency has worked with clients who might be in a similar category or size. Then visit with some of those clients to find out how they were treated, what the agency has done for them, are they pleased, etc.

Finally, you should make sure that the principals of the agency have the experience of the level of company that you want to become. You don't want to change ships halfway on your sail. However, it has to want your business; you don't want the team pitching for the account and get the B team working on it!

12. Create the advertising, communication, and promotional plans for all of the links in the sales chain.
Consistency is the one message that I hope you get out of this part of the book. Many times we get different groups of

agencies or people in-house to work on the various pieces that we use to communicate with our customers. Unfortunately, we can all fall short when it comes to consistency for a myriad of reasons, but I have to tell you that having a creative platform and sticking to it, no matter what, will give you a serious edge over the majority of the competition.

This book is not meant to teach all about advertising communications, but I would suggest that if you are interested in getting more information, then the one book that I would recommend is **Ogilvy on Advertising** by David Ogilvy.

To put the plan together, you should initially do some homework. Check with your trade association or industry media to see what the rest of the category is doing. Now, this is not necessarily what you have to do, but you need this information so that you know what your industry considers to be the norm; it's a good foundation. You should also begin to track whatever your competition is doing. It's fairly easy to see what it is up to—it's all public information. You can get media information by having a service to find out for you, or simply watch for the competition's advertising and promoting in all of the media. Get people who work in your company to be your eyes and ears: They can be local or national, but make sure they all keep aware of what is going on in the marketplace.

Once you have all of the information about what the competition is doing, you should start to build a matrix of all of the various forms of communications it is using. Check out national, regional, and local advertising—this could be TV, radio, print media, billboards, Internet, direct mail, co-op advertising, promotional programs, press releases, premiums or giveaways, incentives, literature, sales brochures, marketing books, telemarketing, trade shows, newsletters, videotapes, CDs, and more.

Once all this is gathered, you can start extending the matrix to include the dates on which the various media and promotional programs occur. The last component is to establish the costs of all of the elements that make up the competition's advertising communication and promotional plan. Now you are in a position to move forward with a plan of your own, based on facts. You now know the general category marketplace, you now know what your immediate competition is doing, so this is the time to put together a plan that will get the maximum awareness of your brand across all of the communication and sales media. The thing is, if you know what your competition's plans were last year, there is a good chance that, all things being equal, they will probably put in place a plan that is very similar this year. (I can't tell you how many major companies I have worked with that get a new brand manager in place yet the only real thing that he or she wants to do is not mess up. So that person basically changes last year's brand marketing plan and ups the spending to match the sales forecast, and that becomes the new plan.)

So now you are acting on the information, not reacting. Your plan can be produced to take advantage of the information; you can now work smarter. For instance, if you have a seasonal product and you noticed that last year the competition placed a ½ page black-and-white ad in the local press one week before Easter, you should consider placing a one-third-page or half-page ad and put it in the press 2 weeks before Easter. Now you are doing 2 things: One, you are preempting your competition, and two, you will get more awareness because of the increased size of your ad.

You have all heard of the expression "Think outside of the box": This is something that you should try to do with your plan. Try to think how your customers get their information. Are they likely to get it from the radio driving to work? Read it in an ad while on the train? Watching TV? Reading a magazine? Put yourself in their place, not yours, and you will get a better idea of where you should advertise or promote.

13. Create a look that will be consistent across all communications and last a lifetime.

As I mentioned at the beginning of the previous section, and it's worth repeating: One of the major areas that you can use to differentiate yourself from the competition is to be absolutely fanatical about the consistency of your message. Also, make sure that the creative look, feel, mood, and tone that carries the message is able to transcend all of the communication vehicles. So many companies fall down in what really is an area that's so easy to maintain consistency—all it takes is the will and want to do it. Your creative look or platform has to be consistent with every piece of communication that you produce—pervasive through the advertising, to the sales presenters, the literature, the trucks, the stationary, consumer and trade promotions, and every single piece of creative and/or printed material that your company might use. Consistency of message will give you a serious competitive advantage, and the good news is that it will not cost you a penny more to make it happen, only a will to make it happen.

It starts with your logo and positioning statement. When you have created them, get a master set completed and send a copy of it to all of the parties that are directly involved with the reproduction process. This is called the company's style guide. Also, send a copy to every member in the company, using it as a rally cry for the brand; let your people know that they are vitally important in the usage of the brand, the position, and the execution of it—no matter where it is used. Try to get your employees to be your brand police; explain why it is so important to have a consistent look in everything the brand does. Ask them to keep their eyes open; maybe offer a free dinner or other incentive to anyone seeing the incorrect usage of the brand logo or positioning statement.

During the creative process, you will find that there are numerous ways in which people try to cut corners and not maintain a consistent look, because it's sometimes just easier—especially if there is more than one group of people involved in developing different communication pieces. Nevertheless, the bottom line is, you must be diligent in your protection of the mood, tone, and look of your brand. As I say in my seminars, it doesn't matter if you are producing a "take-one" leaflet, a "cents-off" coupon, or even a Post-It note—they should all look as though they all come from the same family. Guard your look as if it was your child—it is!

14. Produce all of the materials, including packaging, advertising, promotions, public relations, direct mail, and the rest, to support the individual communication plans.

Depending on the size of your company, there may well be different people handling different aspects of all of the materials or products that carry the creative message. For instance, it might be the shipping department that buys the trucks, and they will probably want to make sure that they get the graphics put on those trucks. You might well have a separate P.R. department or agency, ad advertising agency, a packaging company, a promotions company, an Internet or Web agency, and on and on. Maybe you do all of these things inside your company. The problem is that you will have many different groups of people all vying to make themselves seen as the drivers of the creative support program. In my experience, most of the companies that you will work with are probably good people and want to do a good job for you. However, they also have agendas: to get more of the share of the marketing dollars that you are proposing to spend to support your brand. This makes perfectly good sense, but it is not in the best interest of the brand. Over the years I have tried to get clients of mine to get the various groups together to work as a team. I would like to emphasize to you: The more you can get these various groups to work in the best interest of the brand, the more successful your brand will be. The most important thing is that you absolutely must be the driver of this process—no excuses. I would suggest that you talk to either your internal team, or to the internal and external teams, and clearly demonstrate that you are in charge of where the brand is going, and that all of them have got to be team players for the brand's benefit.

I would like to offer a scenario where the brand wins: Get the various disciplines together off-site, lock them all in a room, and develop a marketing and promotional program that is in the best interest of the brand. All of the players would be hired on a fee basis, and the fee would be negotiated separately. This then would mean that the advertising agency would get paid according to the work it did, not on the amount of media spend, the same would go for the P.R. company and the promotion agency. Premium suppliers would bill on a fee for the work completed, not on the price of the item they purchased. The bottom line is that the look and feel that the brand is trying to communicate has got to be consistent over all of the vehicles involved in the process.

15. Get support from all the people who touch your brand— your sales and internal personnel as well as your customers.

The more that you involve all of your company in the branding process, the better off you are going to be and the more consistent your brand impression will be too. In most companies the only people who are involved in the development of the brand are those in the marketing group. This does not make sense; everyone in the company has to be involved. Maybe not in the developmental stages quite so much, but certainly after the direction has been agreed to, the rest of the company has to buy into the vision and look and be behind what the company is trying to do. The direction should be presented to them so that they can clearly understand the reasons behind the decisions that have been made. Do this in the early stages— the earlier, the better. You will be surprised at the great input you will get from these people, and on top of that, they will be so happy that you have involved them and value their opinions.

Naturally, the salespeople are the closest to your customers, so you have to take their opinions seriously, but in my experience, most of the salespeople just want to get the facts to the customer; not necessarily do they grasp the creative side of what the company is doing. They shouldn't—it's not their job. But heed their words, because they really know what is going on out there. Give them tools that make their jobs easier—make them look good in front of the customers. Make sure that they really understand what the brand stands for, why you have chosen this creative direction—that the objective of developing the brand is to get more sales for today and tomorrow.

I would also recommend that you get your customers involved in the development of your creative look and the overall positioning very early in the process. Usually your customers are helpful; everyone wants to win, and your customers will value that you have actually asked them to get involved in the creative process of your brand. Get as many opinions as you can.

16. Develop a customer-centric organization.

CRM, or Customer Relationship Management, is a hot topic, and I go into it further in the book, but I would like to give a story on how I discovered my version of CRM: Customers Really Matter.

When I was a young boy in England, my parents owned a "mom and pop" store. It was what the trade called a CTN: a confectioner/tobacconist/ newsagent. To me, it was a candy store and more. So that's how I got to be a chocoholic. Imagine being a young boy in a candy store! My mom and dad worked really hard and tried to make the store successful as possible, and they did a pretty good job. The reason I am telling you this is that after thinking back on those years, it has become apparent to me that my Dad was one of the best customer relationship managers I have known. He knew all of his customers by name and welcomed them into the store every single time. Sometimes with a joke, sometimes with a simple hello! He would know every single customer's regular habits. He would have their newspaper or magazine ready for them as they were walking in the door; their cigarettes or tobacco, if they smoked. He knew their families and would always ask in his own way how they were, trying to find out if there was any special event, like a birthday coming up. That way he would be in a position to suggest a certain candy or toy. And as he said, he would give them the opportunity to buy. He didn't try to sell; he just gave them the chance to buy. If he had run out of a certain product that a regular customer wanted, he would make a special trip to the wholesaler and pick up what the person wanted—then even drop it off where the person worked, if they worked locally, or certainly have it ready when they came into the store that evening. He also knew that if a customer came into the store and left their wallet at home, they automatically got credit; he knew they were good for it. Do you think my parents' business was successful? Yes, it was, and primarily because they looked after their customers first.

You should try to think of your business like it was a mom and pop store—know your customers, know who spends most, look after them and make sure that they keep coming back again and again. Let's be honest: One mom and pop store is much like another; they all sell the same products. It's the way you are treated, the way you are made to feel comfortable, *not* the products they serve that makes the difference, that's why you keep coming back.

The expression "customer-centric" has become popular, but all it really means is that you have to make some fundamental decisions about the type of company that you want to own or run. In my opinion, with today's competitive market—in fact, with any market—you have to build your company around what your customers want to buy, not what you want them to buy. It sounds easy, but in reality it is very hard to do, especially when it comes to, for example, supporting a returns policy that has no exceptions, and you are hurting because your shipping department made a big packing mistake and your products are arriving scratched.

We all know the expression "The customer is always right." Well, we know that sometimes they are wrong too. What works is a customer-centric organization that listens, really listens, to what the customers' needs are, instead of worrying about trying to sell them something—and then makes a product or delivers a service that meets those needs. This concept has got to be drilled into your company; everyone has to clearly understand that you don't have a business without customers. No one gets a paycheck without customers, there is no bonus scheme, no retirement program: The customers are the single most important part of your company, and everyone has to get on board the "customer first" concept.

CHAPTER 3

IDENTIFYING YOUR TARGET AUDIENCE

We all know who our customers are, don't we? Are you sure? Sometimes, the best and most profitable customer is not the one you think. The thing is, you have to really make a concerted effort to find out who the best prospects for your brand are and how you can reach them.

In most industries there are accepted demographics of the target audience, and we buy our advertising based on these demographics. For instance, the target might be male, age 35 to 55, college-educated, who works and has 1.5 children at home. Reach and frequency are some of the measurements used, as well as rating points against the target. That's all well and good, but in today's environment you have to go much deeper. You have to know who the individual customer is and certainly what their traits are. When I am working on this part for my clients, we try to establish how our customers spend their days and evenings 7 days a week. We call it "a week in the life of" whoever. Eventually we actually name the fictitious person; as I mentioned in an earlier chapter, this way we can always refer to our target easily, and everyone in the company knows who this "person" is and how they react to our communications. We try to find out what they do when they wake up in the morning: Do they listen to the radio (what station)? Or do they watch TV (what station)? If they work, how do they get there (drive, bus, train)? And do they read the paper or listen to the radio? Again, what do they read? What do they listen to? Do they read trade magazines at work? Where do they go for lunch? Do they drive to the deli or dinner? What time do they do the reverse commute? What do they do when they get home—play with the kids, watch the Little League? Do they read the paper before watching TV? Do they go out during the week, movies, bowling, golf, exercise? And on and on, until you have created a complete week in the life of the ideal customer. Now you can establish all of the multitude of media that is available to reach them under normal or abnormal circumstances, then decide on the media that you think will get the maximum awareness within the budget framework that you have established for the brand.

Oftentimes marketers and consumers look at the same situation, but with different results. Marketers are usually concerned with the marketplace itself (e.g., what stage of growth the product's category is in) and what is their brand's share of market versus the competition's. On the other hand, their customers have a completely different view—in fact, they probably could care less what brand share the brand has, and they really are not interested in whether the brand is achieving its objectives or goals. All they really care about is how the brand affects them, what can it do for them, and will it deliver what they expect of it.

People look at situations in completely different ways. Try to put yourself in the consumer's shoes more often than you do. Think like a consumer does and you will have a much better chance to make your advertising and marketing dollars work, and work harder.

I don't want to overcomplicate this part of bringing your brand to market, but I must tell you that it is vitally important for you to really dig deep to find out who your best prospects are.

I suggest that qualitative research is more important than a numbers-oriented direction. Talking to consumers in small groups—or even better, on a one-on-one basis—will get you a much better feel for the feelings that drive a customer to purchase your brand. It's always hard to see emotion in a report, but emotion is written all over the face of the consumer. GET IN THEIR FACES, GUYS!

Initially, you have to start by looking at the biggest group of potential customers. Once you have done this, I would urge you to start whittling away to the LCD (the lowest common denominator): the individual customer.

In research, there is a system called "segmenting" that is used to sort who the target audience might be. But even segmenting itself is getting reduced, even down to a segment of one, the individual. Take Amazon.com: It now identifies every single visitor. Traditional market research still has its place, and I would really make sure that you use this experience to really listen to the individual consumers that you meet. They might give you the insight into what actually motivates the group you call your target audience.

By the way, when you read the research reports, please try to be somewhat open-minded and read between the lines. When we used to handle the Lipton account, the standing joke was that since research showed that 50% of the country likes hot tea and 50% likes iced tea, should we bring out a Lukewarm Tea brand? Or how many times have you been asked to fill out a questionnaire in a mall or on a plane and filled out the answers totally honestly? Most of us are guilty of exaggerating our salaries either up or down, how many times we fly, or whatever. All I am saying is, treat the research with the respect it deserves; it is not an exact science.

There are now quicker ways to get your research questions answered other than the traditional focus group concept. There are now companies that have developed what has been called "virtual research": It uses America Online customers to talk about what their true feelings are about a brand. Oftentimes they will get so much more information than in a focus group situation. Another concept is photo sorting: Basically, it gets consumers to sort photos into the groups or types of people the photos represent to them. They are asked to sort photos into what their perception is of different brands. Another research method is known as ethnography—following consumers around in their own environment and filming their every move (well, not their **every** move)!

Finally, there is a special group of people who I respect called planners that work within the advertising industry. Their job is specifically to represent the consumer in all of the conversations or during the creative process at the advertising agency. An ad agency in London created the original concept of planning. (It also happened to be the same agency that I originally sold my company to, Boase Messimi Pollit, now known as BMP/DDB.) Probably one of the best planners in the industry is John Steele, who wrote a book called **Truth, Lies and Advertising;** if you are interested in the planning process, it's a must-read.

I know this is probably an awful lot of information about research, but what I want you to remember is that you should use every piece of research available to you. Make sure that you talk to your customers, and listen—really listen—to what they have to say, then develop your marketing plans based upon what will really impact your customers and what will help them increase your business.

CHAPTER 4

BRANDING TO THE BONE

In the introduction I described visual impressions that really illustrate what branding inside your company is all about, first with the stick of Rock story. It's so important to ensure that your employees, from the top to the bottom, are on the same wavelength as you are when it comes to your brand. I talked a little earlier about developing a Brand Commitment Statement, and not only you, but everyone, should be able to quote it word for word at any time. **Developing the Brand Commitment Statement** should be fairly easy: It's putting into words what you want your brand to mean to your company, the people in it, and the people who buy your products. Maybe you could make it into a competition within the company; perhaps giving a prize to the person that comes up with the winning statement. The good thing about such a method is that it will get everyone involved in the process and clearly demonstrate that they are all part of that process.

Everyone in the company has to know where you stand and what the company stands for too! The Brand Commitment Statement can accomplish both of these goals for you. This is not a Mission Statement, which states primarily what the company wants to achieve and the manner in which it wishes to conduct itself on that journey. A Brand Commitment Statement is what you want the brand to mean internally and externally. It also represents a way to allow your employees to act on behalf of the best interests of the company: what the company expects of itself and what it wants to deliver to its customers.

One of the most important factors in getting your brand message across on a consistent basis is having the right personnel to invoke it. Most companies have people that are considered key employees; these are the ones who you know you just really would not want to be without. The problem is that you don't have many of them; they are good, but they are not deep in your business. This then becomes an opportunity to make a difference by getting the rest of your company to match the caliber of the key employees. If yours is like most companies, it will be working on the 20–60–20 concept: The first 20% of the company are superstars: These are the **key group** of employees, these are the ones that would really hurt the company if they quit. The second group, about 60% are the **engine group** of the company, are really good people but just not superstars. The final 20% are the group that I call the "**nomads**": They are just there, they turn up and do something, and get a paycheck. By correcting this concept, getting rid of the nomads and making it into a 25–75 or 30–70 situation using only key and engine groups, it becomes a huge opportunity to differentiate yourselves from the competition—you just have to find out where and who these additional people are. We have all heard of headhunters, and I have asked a friend of mine Abbe Walter, who is a hugely successful headhunter in Washington, D.C., to compile a hiring process document that lists all of the questions you should ask and how you should conduct the interview. This is it, and it can also be seen as an attachment at the end of the book.

The Hiring Process
Hiring is a process, not an act!

Things to do when hiring personnel:

The person you hire will determine the results you get on the job! Before you start your candidate search, IDENTIFY YOUR NEEDS. Consider how this person will fit in the bigger picture: company culture, management style, existing employees, what the job specifications are.

CANDIDATE SEARCH

Establish a good working relationship with your recruiter/search firm. This will save you lots of time—a good recruiter should have a solid understanding of more than just the skills you need and what your company does: He/she should know the culture and personality of your firm. Recruiters should be able to identify talent even when there is no open position and bring the candidate to your attention.

INTERVIEWING

The GOAL of interviewing is more than just gathering facts: You want a clear picture of past accomplishments and track record, how he/she will handle different situations, how their past experience will transfer over to your company. Define your hiring goals, know what you are looking for in a candidate, and then develop a predetermined list of questions that should change for different jobs. This will maintain consistency in interviewing all candidates.

LET THE CANDIDATE DO MORE OF THE TALKING!!!!

A common mistake by an employer not used to interviewing is to tell the candidate too much initially about what the job requires and what the company is looking for…this allows the candidate to answer with what they think the employer wants to hear. Your job as the interviewer is to listen and evaluate.

DON'T ask many yes/no questions—ask open-ended questions; situational and behavioral questions like:

Tell me about a time when...

How would you handle this situation...

Describe your most significant accomplishment...

Describe the culture/philosophy of your former firms...

Make sure the candidate explains the structures of his past firms and how they fit into the picture—you need to determine if they are applicable to your firm.

CONTROL THE INTERVIEW—your time is valuable. Once you determine a candidate is not suitable, do NOT feel obligated to spend a lot of time with them.

REFERENCES are so important; many employers do not thoroughly check references. References can help determine what the previous employer's methods of measuring performance were and how the company is similar to or different from yours. A candidate who was a good fit with one firm may not necessarily be a good fit for yours. It is important through interviewing and reference checking to get a sense of the past employer's organizational structure.

GET AT LEAST 3 PEOPLE IN YOUR ORGANIZATION TO INTERVIEW THE CANDIDATE! The interviewers don't have to be from the department that is going to hire, but a completely different perspective will come from this exercise. It also involves more than one department and shows the current employees that you value their input.

OVERALL, MAKE SURE THAT YOU CONDUCT AN ONGOING SEARCH FOR TALENTED PEOPLE WHO WILL ENHANCE AND GROW YOUR COMPANY. These people are out there; you just have not managed to find them yet.

FINALLY, make sure that you conduct ongoing reviews about your employees; the biggest problem of most companies is that they "hire in haste and fire at leisure." Remember, the people who are usually looking for jobs are in the bottom quartile of the talent pool. So when you suddenly find out that you are going to lose a valuable **employee, you will only get applications from the people who are currently looking. And there is usually a reason for that!**

A couple of hiring thoughts that I would like you to consider are: *Hire slowly and fire quickly* and *"I will" attitude beats IQ every time*. We should be more concerned with a continuing hiring process, because that is what it should be—hiring should be a process, not an act! In addition, always hire people who give you the promise that they will get a job done: It's far better to have someone who says "I'll do that" rather than "I *can* do that"! I hope that the hiring process document will help show you how to ask what questions to ask and not to ask, as well as give you tips that will make you a better interviewer; and most importantly of all, it will tell you to "ask questions and listen." That advice was given to me many years ago by a friend and probably the best speaker I have ever heard on selling, Jack Daly. The "ask questions and listen" mode of selling is particularly hard for those of us who tend to sell using the "verbal diarrhea" method. It took me a long time to really get it; one day I was talking to my wife, who happens to be a doctor, and I suddenly realized that doctors exemplified the "ask questions and listen" concept better than any other group. That's what they do for a living: They just ask, and until you have finished talking, they are unable to make any decisions as to what is best for you.

You probably hold many meetings in your company: sales meetings, production meetings, accounting meetings, marketing meetings, and so on, but how many brand meetings do you have? I would suggest that if you want to get more brand awareness in your company, then you have to make your employees more brand-aware. It takes a lot of effort to do it right, but think that it will give you a distinct advantage to do it while your competitors are not doing it. Get your people involved in disseminating the brand positioning statement: They must know what you intend to be and to mean to your customers, suppliers, and the rest of the staff. Something that will really help is if at the end of every meeting, regardless of the type of meeting, you ask the question, "How does what we are doing affect the brand?" Try doing this in every meeting for the next year if you want to raise brand awareness internally and externally. Increasing the brand awareness internally will also get your staff in the mode of thinking about not only the brand, but sales too. Every person in the company, in addition to being a brand ambassador, is a salesperson too!

Think of the opportunities: Every employee is asked "What do you do?" or "Where do you work?" at sometime or another; if yours have been given the branding tools, then the response will come out the way that you want it. Your accounting department probably speaks to their equivalent positions at your suppliers and to customers alike—think of the opportunities they have to ask questions and receive the answers. For instance, "How are we doing on deliveries? Do you have any problems with things breaking or getting scratched in transit? Do we get our goods to you on time? What do our competitors do for you that we don't? Roughly how much of your business are we getting versus the competition?" Because your accounting department and theirs are kind of "on the same team", they will give this kind of information willingly, and it is invaluable. All you have to do is train your people to ask the questions. The same applies to the delivery person, the receptionist, manufacturing, and on through as many departments that you have. Get them all involved in the running and promoting of the brand; they will get a pride of ownership that will be hard to beat.

One way that you can improve the performance level of your personnel and any promotional programs is by making sure that you measure them and reward people on these results:

HOW DO YOU KNOW IF YOUR BRAND IS ON TRACK?

Here are some questions that you should ask yourself to know if your brand is on track; answer on a scale of 1 to 10. Keep the answers, then take the same test 6 months from now and compare the answers, to see whether there is improvement.

1. Can you describe your brand in a few words? You should be able to communicate this easily—it should just roll off your tongue. I am sure you have all heard of the "elevator speech." If you and your employees can't do it, then work at developing one so that the recipient—the customer—will get it.

2. How many in your potential target audience have any awareness of your product category and your brand specifically?

3. When consumers shop the category, is your brand the brand purchased most often?

4. Are your brand's claims defensible, or can they be challenged? For instance, British Airways has a tag line "the world's favorite airline"; this is a fact and is defensible: British Airways flies more people to more destinations than any other airline in the world.

5. Can your customers easily identify your brand from the competition in your marketplace? Does it have a USP (unique selling proposition)?

6. Will customers pay what you think your product is worth? Will they pay a premium price for your brand?

7. Is your brand timeless? In other words, are there claims or time-specific elements in your brand name that could affect the longevity? When we developed the Sims Freeman O'Brien name, we deliberately chose not to have a tag line or positioning statement until we were absolutely certain of what we wanted to be to our target audience.

8. Does the brand really deliver the benefits your customers are looking for?

9. Is your product or service relevant in today's marketplace; is the category in a growth or declining phase?

10. Are you communicating your brand's image with consistent and multiple quality impressions?

11. Does your brand have a better (e.g., premium) position in consumers' minds than your competitors' brands do?

12. Is your brand delivering a consistent image across all communications?

13. Are you making sure that the brand is being featured in all of the media that is effective in reaching your target audience?

14. How well do you know who your customers are? Do you know what they like and don't like? Do you know what they look like and what motivates them?

15. Do you audit your marketing programs to ensure their efficiency?

The chances are that you answered no to question 15, so what follows is a series of questions that you might want to consider, following your next promotional program that you put into the marketplace:

1. Key factors that impacted your business for good or bad during past years, including an evaluation of marketing surprises.

2. Customer satisfaction based on research among key target groups.

3. Distributor, vendor, or intermediary satisfaction.

4. Marketing knowledge, attitudes, and satisfaction of all executives involved in the marketing function.

5. The extent to which the marketing program was marketed internally, and bought into, by top management and non-marketing executives.

6. The extent to which each decision in the marketing mix— e.g., targeting, positioning, pricing, advertising, etc.— was made correctly after evaluating many alternatives in terms of profit-related criteria.

7. The performance of advertising, promotion, sales force, and marketing research programs, with an emphasis on return-on-investment issues.

8. Whether the marketing plan achieved its stated financial goals and objectives.

9. Which aspects of the plan failed to meet the objectives, together with specific recommendations for improving next year's performance.

10. The current value of brand equity for each brand in the product portfolio.

*Reproduced with permission of Copernicus Marketing

One of the most effective tools that I have ever used for companies who are serious about growing their brands is to form a **Dealer Council** for 2-step distribution brands or **Customer Council** if you sell directly. This is the one area that you can count on coming out a winner, even if the only news you get is bad—at least you know what you have to do to put it right. However, in all of my experience, I have never known any company or group to not come out saying that it is probably one of the best things we have ever done to grow the business. It's easy to do: Just invite 6 or more, up to about 12, of your direct customers; by that, I mean the next step in the sales chain, if you are in a two-step distribution product category. For this example, let's call them dealers: those who sell your product to the consumers. First of all, you need to establish what you want to get out of the meeting and then put the information down in writing. Then you can put together a list of questions that you would like answered by your dealers. (I have included a set of questions in the appendix of this book that you might want to at least consider.)

Next is getting the group together; I suggest taking them off-site, maybe to a hotel, just so there is complete focus on the job at hand. The very fact that you are asking these people to participate in the dealer council, recognizing them as experts in the industry, will pay off to the participants. The group should be made up of some of your best customers, a couple of fence-sitters, and maybe a couple of potential customers. They should have been given the questions ahead of time and come to the meeting with their answers to the questions. This will save you a great deal of time for the day.

   Start the session with thanks to the attendees and get the people to introduce themselves. Then go through the questions and get everyone to read their answers. You can ask many more questions for which you would like to get group input, show the marketing plan that you want to put into place, and maybe show a new product that you want to bring to market. The best part is that you are going to get a group of people who will feel that they are special customers, like experts, and want to participate in making you successful. They will also go and tell friends of the experience and how you are really trying to become a customer-friendly, customer-centric company. I would suggest that you conduct at least 2 a year and maybe rotate some of the attendees; it can't help to get more people exposed to the "council" concept.

GROW YOUR BRAND "SENSIBLY"!
   A number of years ago I was developing a branding seminar for one of my clients. They had heard all of the standard information that you normally get in "branding books," so I tried to look at another way that we could improve the brand experience by the customer. I came up with the idea that we normally understand about brands through a *visual* medium (TV, print), and because the big brand names are able to spend more money in these areas, they then are able to keep or increase their share of market. What we do not do is maximize and take opportunities with the other 4senses we have—**touch, sound, taste, and smell!**

   The sight or visual medium is what we normally associate with the communication or promotion P (see 5 P's of Branding, Total Branding, and the Branding Wheel in chapter 5). Our visuals communicate the impression that we are trying to make and should be persuasive in getting our target audience to consider or purchase our product. Please remember what I have said before: You must make sure that they are consistent, and with multiple quality impressions, across all of the materials produced: TV, print, trucks, letterheads, etc.!

Branding through **touch or feel** is a sense that is not normally thought of too much in the branding process, but it really is extremely important. Feel is invoked in 2 ways—first, the feel of the product itself: How many times have you seen a woman going through a department store just feeling clothes on a rack? It has to feel good to her before she even considers looking at the item. How does a cashmere sweater feel, a soft leather jacket, the smooth feel of a Bang & Olufson stereo, a top-quality piece of stationery?

The other feel is the emotional feeling you get when you think of or even use the brand. This is an area where you can get a big jump over the competition if you spend enough time on the aesthetics and quality of your product. Think about how you would feel if you were wearing a Swatch watch; it would make you feel a little sporty and it would tell the time for you. But what happens if you are wearing a Rolex or a Cartier; how do you feel now about the watch on your wrist? Emotional feelings are vital to your brand becoming successful. This is the moment of truth—when a consumer is going to take money out of their wallet to buy your category, and at that moment it has to be a good emotional move for them to make to become a truly satisfied customer.

Sound or hearing is a vital ingredient in the Total Branding concept. We normally think of radio as the sound part of the communication mix, but it's far more than that. First, of course, listen to what your customers, employees, and suppliers have to say. Ask them often, and go as deep as you can—and the listening should be done by you and your employees as much as possible, not outside agencies. Other forms of sound are the way the brand or product actually performs. A few years ago, Harley-Davidson tried to trademark the sound of their bikes. There is no mistaking the sound certain cars make; when I was young I used to love hearing the sound of a British car called an MGB because it had such a distinctive sound—that was its best advertising. There is a sound that a Jaguar car makes when you shut the door; the sound of the click of a lock on a fine piece of furniture; the sound that Intel makes in the commercials that it participates in. How many commercials can you think of where the sound, rather than the word or visuals, actually made you think of the brand, such as the McDonald's "We love to see you smile," NBC's three-note bell, or Sprint's pin-drop sound and visual?

Taste can be experienced in 2 ways. First is the actual taste of the product; the other is the level of "taste" that a brand enjoys. Taste of a product is an incredible differentiation between brands. Think of Godiva chocolates, McDonald's french fries, your favorite cocktail. We have to make sure that the taste is used to maximize the brand experience. **Taste** can also mean *class*, and can be seen in the way you produce your communications message. As guardians of the brand, you should expect to create communications that exceed the level of taste that the target audience expects of you. Taste comes through in the fabrics you use to communicate the message, the way you and your employees carry yourselves at a trade meeting, every one of you looking and conducting yourself better than the competition. One of the best examples I can think of is how Muhammad Ali not only considered himself "the greatest," but he also made sure that he looked the greatest, because he always dressed the part. Other than when he was training, you just would not see him without a suit, white shirt, and tie—he believed that he should look like a champion in every way! Other examples are Lexus introducing itself to us with a rose on the seat when we first bought their car or Mercedes giving you lifetime road assistance. This type of taste makes it very difficult for your competition to beat you—always keep the taste level of your brand at the highest level possible.

Smell is another way of a brand differentiating itself from the competition; just think about the success that Cinnabon has enjoyed throughout the malls of America. Starbucks, of course, has done an incredible job in their coffee shops, not only with smell, but with the taste of the product and the various surroundings they are seen in. The smell of the leather in your new Cadillac or new purse, the wood on your new table—all have distinct smells that make you feel good about the brand.

You may not be able to use all of the senses directly in your brand, but at least consider using them in the ways you want your customers to enjoy the brand experience. Maybe it is the paper you use in your stationery. The way you send a written thank-you note—maybe the note even smells like the leather of the car's interior that you sell or the perfume you stock! You get the idea—don't be close-minded about using all of our senses. It could well be one of the ways that you can build your brand into a leader.

CHAPTER 5

TOTAL BRANDING—THE 5 P'S

Let's talk about the structure of a brand and what goes into its makeup. If you've taken Marketing 101 at college, you've heard of the 4 P's of marketing: **Product, Price, Placement, and Promotion.** These tools have stood the test of time; they have certainly worked for the Proctor & Gambles and other major manufacturers of this world. Keeping the 4 P's in mind, I wanted to create a phrase that would easily remind you of how a brand is developed across all aspects of the communication and manufacturing process. I have developed a brand concept overview that I call **Total Branding and The Branding Wheel,** and it will remind us of what branding really consists of. The outside of the wheel are the 4 areas that we talked about at the beginning of the book. Making a branding PROMISE and *keeping it.* Your customers' branding EXPECTATION: *Meet or exceed it.* Getting a bigger share of your customer's mind when they are shopping your brand category: *Earn it.* And as for getting a bigger share of their wallet when they are buying the brand category: *Deserve it.*

The spokes of the wheel are the 5 P's of Branding, and they are **Product, Placement, Promotion, People, and Passion.** The differences between the marketing concept and the branding concept are **PEOPLE** and **PASSION,** because people affect the brand more than any other area, and they also deliver the passion. Yes, people make the difference—not money, not price. Price is always a factor, but price has no emotion, no feelings, no trust, no needs, no desire, and no ego, all of which are the major factors in the purchasing decision.

A wheel diagram with BRAND at the center, surrounded by spokes labeled: EXPECTATION, PASSION, SHARE OF WALLET, PROMOTION, PROMISE, PRODUCT, PLACEMENT, SHARE OF MIND, PEOPLE.

I assume that you all drive a car. So without trying to be too hard on any manufacturer, how many of you drive a Yugo? If you said yes, well, good for you: It's a good, practical car that will get the job done. It's got 4 wheels, a heater, a spare wheel, and it's cheap. It has everything that you need to get you from A to B and can go faster than the speed limit allows, so why would you buy anything else? Because to most of you, the Yugo just doesn't satisfy what you are looking for in a car; it doesn't meet the criteria that you have set. It certainly has all of the basic attributes that are necessary in a car, but it probably doesn't meet the criteria that you have established for yourself. You have hopes, dreams, aspirations, wants, and needs that you'd like in a car's features and benefits. Maybe a "basic" is that it doesn't make you look as good as you want: You want your neighbors and workmates to like your car; it's a badge that states who you are in society. The net result is that while the Yugo gets the job done, it doesn't satisfy what you are looking for in a car, and you will pay more money to achieve these objectives and look good to the world around you!

The Total Branding concept is probably the single most important aspect that you have to consider when growing your brand into a brand leader. In the Branding Wheel, it shows how the brand, the customer, and you should be in the center of your thinking about the way you go to business—it's a way of life! The items that are listed under the 5 P's are generic; you can add more items that are relevant to your product category. However, I just cannot emphasize enough how important it is to make your brand #1 in your category; you have to believe and invoke this thinking into your business, and that's the passion.

All 5 P's are important, but some are more important than others. If you don't have a passion for your brand, frankly, the other 4 P's just won't happen! You have got to let your passion for your brand, your product, the people around you show—your passion has to permeate throughout your organization, become infectious!

Passion: Let me reinforce how important having a passion about your brand is. The passion has to start at the top and trickle down through the corporation—if you are the president or CEO, then you have to be the brand hero. Why on earth would your people get behind the brand unless they see you leading the charge? Passion is infectious, and you want your people, customers, and suppliers to know you are insistent upon your brand being handled with care, consistent in its message, and delivering the product quality in the way that you want it.

We were once trying to get a piece of business from the Jell-O brand at General Foods, and I knew that we were in a pitch situation with 4 other companies. After looking at the final 3 campaigns that we wanted to present to the client, I felt comfortable that we had produced the best work that we could. But there was still something missing. While the work was good enough, in my opinion, to win the shootout, it did not convey the passion of how we felt about wanting to win the business. I knew that the competition was going to be tough, our work was great, but I wanted to make sure that we sent the client a very strong message that we were passionate about wanting to earn and keep their business. The project was for a special promotion geared toward the Texas market, and I think you know how passionate Texans are about Texas. So when 2 of us went in to present to the very staid General Foods group, we drew some incredible stares. We were completely dressed like cowboys, chaps, spurs, the whole 9 yards. If we had not won the project and eventually the account, you know I would not be writing about it here. Sometimes you just have to show the customers that you have the passion—you really want their business! I am not suggesting that you dress up like clowns or cowboys, but I am suggesting that you must really let your customers know how much you appreciate their business and that you want to earn it on a continuing basis.

People: *Employees, dealers, end users, vendors, friends, and the rest of the world!*

People are involved in every step of the production of your product or service: your employees, dealers, distributors, end users, vendors, friends, and the rest of the world—**they are the brand**. Every employee—from the people in the accounting department to those in shipping, research, legal, marketing, on the shop floor and throughout the company—represents the brand. It's not just the salesperson that matters! As I mentioned earlier, your accounting department calls someone in the client's accounting department on a regular basis. Maybe it's to chase money; maybe it's to clear up a billed consignment that got lost. This is a chance for your accounting person to get a little closer and find out how your company is doing with them, **the**

customers. It's a great opportunity to get inside information: How are we doing? Why do you think is competition is getting the lion's share of the business? How can we do a better job at your company? And many other questions that you would like answered. I would go so far as to try to get these 2 people together—give them the opportunity to get closer, let them go out to lunch on you. It will pay back dividends in the long run. Remember the "stick of Rock" concept that I mentioned in the beginning of the book—how the name of the town is presented through the candy? Try to keep that visual impression in mind—that's how your company has to make Total Branding work.

Product: *Variety, quality, design, features, brand name, packaging, sizes, services, warranties, returns, research*

Your product is not only a functional product or service, but it should also be a continual reminder and reinforcement of your brand positioning to the customer. In product, the way you decide what you bring to market, how many varieties, the quality and standards that you manufacture to—all dramatically impact the consumer's experience. One way that I believe can make a difference between us, and our competition, is to spend more time in the design stage of the physical product or service. Design can be the printed piece to the physical manufactured product. Unfortunately, we do not spend anywhere near enough time on the design of the physical product in the U.S. compared to our European counterparts. We tend to make sure that whatever we are producing is functionally OK. I would suggest that if you are going to the trouble of creating a functional product, why not make it a great design too?

The product itself is probably one of the best marketing tools you have. Anytime the consumer recommends your product to someone else who is in your purchasing set, it's the highest endorsement you can get. Approximately 70% of all sales start from a recommendation from a friend or associate. The total customer experience—including follow-up customer services and even how you deal with returns—can have a dramatic effect on the customer experience and long-term relationship and growth of your brand.

Here's something that I would suggest you do on an annual basis: **Blow your company up!** (I mean that figuratively.) Get your key employees together and go off-site and have a meeting that is dedicated to starting your business from scratch, as if you were working form a clean sheet of paper. Believe me, most of your people will come up with great ideas that they have probably been thinking about anyway but have not had the opportunity to discuss with you. Go through all of their ideas and make sure that you focus on the idea of what makes it better for the customer, not for you and your company and its employees. If you don't do this, someone else in your category will!

Placement: *Distribution, locations, stores, transportation, production facilities*

These are generic headings, and you may well be able to add more that are pertinent to your specific industry. I want you to imagine that all of these areas are like a full-page advertisement for your company. They should all have a communications message consistent with the rest of the campaign approach you're developing/planning/building. I know this seems somewhat unusual, but every single piece of communication affects the end user or consumer in some way, shape, or form. For instance, you expect FedEx to have consistency in its trucks, boxes, envelopes, and the uniforms its delivery people wear. But even if it produced an unusual promotion (let's say, a "$2 off" voucher), then you would also expect the voucher to look like and fit in with everything else it produces. In other words, you would not be surprised by something out of the norm, because it would still look as though it belonged.

When it comes to your company, it is not only the logo on your trucks, it's also the logo on the driver's shirt, the cleanliness of the truck, and the way in which the delivery person interacts with the customer that count. They should look the way you want them to look and act the way you want, speak the way you want your brand image to be communicated, and generally deliver the brand promise. This should all be scripted, leaving nothing to chance or choice. **They are your brand image.** Think about your last visit to a Disney park. Nothing there is left to chance. All of the people who work there understand that it has to be the Disney way or the highway! Next time you are in a Disney park, check out the nail heads; every single nail head has the mouse logo on it. Every person who works there is scrubbed clean—no tattoos, no body piercings—and look like clean-cut, all-American people. This is not a coincidence; it is a deliberate—and successful—effort to make you feel at home.

Promotion: *Essence, image, advertising, sales promotion, direct mail, public relations, sales force, marketing, outdoor advertising, and Internet advertising*

This is the area we think of most when discussing brand and brand impression. This covers the vast area of communication of the very essence of the brand image: advertising, sales promotion, direct mail, Internet advertising, public relations, marketing sales force, and point of sale. There are so many different elements that would take several books to cover each, but remember—consistency should run through all of the promotion's components. Sometimes you don't have to have a great design—as long as you are consistent with it and with the message, you will be ahead of the competition. I cover how to create a promotion for your brand later in the book, but the overall image and impression that you are trying to communicate must have a look and feel, pervasive throughout everything you create, that communicates with internal personnel, suppliers, sales forces, customers, and end users.

Total Branding affects each one of the 5 P's, and each of the 5 P's affects the brand in its own way. I urge you to keep on your office wall a copy of the chart to remind you of how the 5 P's and the branding wheel work throughout your business and your brand. If you are the CEO, president, or leader of your company's marketing team, then I urge you to get into the center position and make sure that you are in control of all these efforts. Most people think they are doing this, but in my experience, they are only paying lip service to this notion. Your brand is vital to your success, more today than ever. The economy is on a roller coaster, and people are demanding lower prices, but at the end of the day, the consumer will always pay a premium price for a quality product.

It can't be overemphasized how important it is to keep the brand concept overview in mind. So many times, in my work as a consultant, I've seen internal politics get in the way of creating a brand and customer-centric organization. You are the leader of your company, so if you want to become a leading brand, then you have to be the brands leader. Lead your people in bringing branding into everything you and your company does.

CHAPTER 6

16 BRANDING MUSTS

To grow a brand, you have to have many support elements. However, if you follow the 16 steps to launch a brand, incorporate the Total Branding Concept, and use the following 16 Branding Musts, you will be well on your way to creating a brand leader. These "Musts" have been developed from years of experience, and I know that if you implement them, your brand and your bottom line will benefit for the long haul.

1. The brand identity is how you would like the brand to be perceived, but only the customer's image of your brand is real, and that's the only one that counts.

The most important thing to remember when you're discussing and developing your brand's image is how you would like it to be seen. This is its identity, its image; it's the position at which we would like our target audience to think about us. We all know what brand identity is: We used to know it as "corporate identity," and that still is a very important part of the brand's total communications package. But there is also the emotional involvement and the promise that the consumer expects for the brand to have its maximum effect. While the Nike story has been told many times, it's still worth going through the following exercise. Everyone knows the "Swoosh" logo: It reminds us of Nike, and Nike reminds us to "Just Do It," 3 elements that together reinforce the brand. Let's take it one step forward: When you think of Nike, my guess is that the following thoughts go through your mind: You feel that Nike makes a good quality product, they make you look good, it's value for money, and you will probably pay a little bit more for it. Isn't that what you want for your brand—customers feeling that you make a good product, they are prepared to pay a premium price for it, and you make them look good while they still have value for money. Remember that it's how you would like the brand to be seen—that, of course, has to be the long-term objective, and you should always stick with your message. *But the bottom line is that it's what customers think about the brand that's really important, and how close you can get them to thinking about your product or service positioning statement.* That is something you should make sure you find out, and frankly, the only way to do that is ask! You should *always* perform "Brand to the Bone" market research about your customers. As I mentioned earlier, you should conduct conventional market research, but you have to go one step further—go deeper. There are things that you can't see in a market research report: You can't see the consumers' eyes move, you can't see them shrug their shoulders, you can't see them look at their partners, and you can't hear anything beyond the standard answers supplied by a questionnaire. Not only must you learn to read between the lines and put the research you're reading in perspective, you have to go out and talk to your prospective customers yourself. You simply can't beat getting in front of your customers to get a real feel for what's going on.

2. Keep your brand focused; don't try to be all things to all people.

When you're starting to develop your product's branding and advertising, keep the KISS concept in mind. Make the communications meaningful but focused. You can't be all things to all people; you have to take a leadership position and decide what your company is. If you have been developing your brand for some time, make sure that your communication mix is kept simple and that it talks directly to your target audience.

For instance, some of the dot-com advertising you've seen has been real breakthrough stuff, but did it cause people to put their hands in their pockets and part with money? Did it move the sales needle? No! A lot of those companies are now in the dot-com cemetery. Why did a lot of these companies fail? I think it's because they got caught up in their own press; they were legends in their own minds before they even got started. They were trying to impress the wrong audience; they were appealing to the financial and category communities. They disregarded the fact that they were a business like any other business, and like any other business, they needed to be based on a strong foundation. And that is: a good product, an identifiable and reachable target audience, a great marketing plan, the people to take their product to market, and the financial support to keep it going. Don't make the same mistake! **You cannot develop a brand at warp speed, no matter what some experts tell you. A strong brand is built over time.** It's not like the old TV show ***Bewitched;*** you can't just twitch your nose and make it happen. Just a few years ago a company by the name of Pixelon decided to launch their company with a $16 million party in Las Vegas. This used up over 80% of the venture capital they had raised. Can you imagine doing something like that? They were just trying to impress their trade audience and the financial markets, not their potential customers. They themselves were impressed with the hype that had preceded their launch. They forgot to find out if this event would actually move the sales needle. It is simply irresponsible. Sometimes the slow tortoise does win the race and stays in the game for a long time. In branding, slow and steady usually wins.

Now is the time to remember the "Stick of Rock" concept and how it should embody your whole company. Keeping your brand focused also means knowing that everyone who works with you is part of the building of your brand because, in their own areas, they all deliver a message about your brand. The receptionist—who greets you with a cheery message, remembers your customers' names, and, even better, recognizes their voices on the phone—he or she delivers the first impression of your brand every time when answering the phone. **Make sure the receptionist is trained and works from your script to ensure that he or she represents your brand in the manner in which**

you want it represented. If you call Durasol, you will be answered by a pleasant voice saying, "It's a great day at Durasol. May I help you?" Now, it's not an **average** day at Durasol, it's a **great** day at Durasol. That's scripted. That's how it's said every time, because we want to make sure that everyone who calls Durasol gets a real feeling that their call is welcome and that Durasol is a company they're going to want to do business with. So make sure that the words used are yours, not theirs. Make the message cheerful, upbeat, and convey a happy, pleasant place to call. Make sure that your answering machine, voice mail, and e-mail all reflect an upbeat and friendly impression, which you want to become your trademark. These are very useful tools that tell a potential your company is efficient and will be a pleasure to deal with. They are free advertising billboards. Put them to work for you.

3. Shoemaker, stick to your last.

A shoemaker's last is the metal piece that a shoe manufacturer or shoe repairer puts on the shoe in order to do the repairs. When the shoe's held fast by a last, he can hammer a new sole into place. Hence, "Shoemaker, stick to your last"—in other words, keep doing what you are doing, and do it well. Whatever product you make, stick to it and don't try to be what you are not. I have often seen companies start moving away from their base product, usually under advice sources that really do not have the expertise to advise them correctly, thus causing irreparable damage. Now, I don't mind line extensions or variations on the same product category, or even products that are aimed at the same target audiences, but **don't** get into areas that you have no expertise in. Leave them to the folks who are already there.

The way to success is to make a product you are really good at and make it the best it can possibly be. The problem is that eager and enthusiastic entrepreneurs start branching out into product categories that, if they were being realistic, they'd know that they know nothing about! Let's take Amazon.com as an example. It is in the Internet books category and has recently branched out aggressively into other areas, like CDs, movies, electronic games, and even some non-entertainment—that is, unrelated—areas, like tools and hardware and kitchen and houseware items. It is achieving huge sales numbers and still not making a profit. In my opinion, it should stay focused on books; it is spreading itself too thin. At the time of writing it only has around a 5% share of the book market, though it has an unequaled opportunity to own the category worldwide. It is losing the opportunity to become the brand leader in books—the place America turns to first when making a book purchase.

4. Dollar-cost average your brand.

A brand is something that will carry you and your employees forward for many years, so make sure you treat it with kid gloves and a great deal of respect. Look after it financially, even when your accountants are telling you to cut back.

One of the biggest mistakes a company can make is to cut back on its advertising, marketing, and branding funding when things are going wrong in its business category. That's totally the wrong way to go. Bad times present a huge opportunity to get brand share at a bargain-basement price.

The financial community usually advises clients to "dollar-cost average investing" to get the safest and most profitable return on investments. I advise you to take the same approach in your advertising marketing and branding: Dollar-cost average your brand investing to get you the safest and most profitable returns. I realize that this does take discipline and courage, but believe me when I tell you, it means you will get a bigger bang for those bucks than you ever thought possible!

Whatever products or service you provide, all the competition in your category will probably be going through the same financial crunch you are. So don't you think that they'll be getting the same advice from their advisers? If you presume that this is in fact the case, then this could categorically be the best time for your brand to get a significant brand-share increase, at a price per point of increase that is far less cost than you would have projected it to be.

I am not saying that you should incrementally spend (unless you have unlimited funds), but what I am saying is that you should continue to spend at the level you had projected. Your return on investment will dramatically exceed any other annual expenditure you will make in your communication spending.

Remember, when the market is hurting, it's usually the cheapest time to generate superior brand awareness and gain market share simply because of the reduction in competitive activities. Also, by investing in the brand wisely and consistently, the payback will come over the long haul. It seems that the first cutbacks are always in advertising and marketing. In my book, cutbacks are the time to put the hammer down—to spend wisely on getting brand share. It's a huge opportunity to separate yourself from your competition.

The American Business Media group examined the relationship between advertising and sales during severe market downturns and found that companies that did not cut advertising and marketing dollars had the highest growth in sales and net income in the 2 years studied and the 2 years following. Companies that cut advertising and marketing dollars had the lowest sales and profit increases during the same periods. During the last downturn Nike increased its spending by 25% and gained a whopping 900% return on its investment. That's being bold, but that's what it takes to be a brand leader: Be bold when others are backing off.

5. When you're starting out, think "street smart."

When you start out, you probably don't think of your business as a brand—but it is, albeit embryonic, and you have to treat it as such. In those early days, you'll be in the period I like to call the "go-go" times. You just go go go all the time, working every hour God gave you and doing every job that has to be done. During this period of growth, as a marketing guy, I would tell you to try and leverage every dollar you have apportioned to advertising and promotion. **Think guerrilla tactics.** Look for ways to spend your small pile of dollars that will give you maximum returns on your investment. Get your name in the free local press, support your local charities, sponsor a Little League team, put leaflets under windshield wipers (if that's appropriate), and give free talks to the local chamber of commerce. Get yourself seen in any way you can. Find unusual ways that will get you brand awareness—but whatever you do, make sure that you have absolute consistency in your message and in the impression it delivers. Never forget that consistency over time builds a brand and its image.

6. When you have a big ad budget, following the advice in #5.

After a while, you may have become a sizable company and able to hire an advertising agency. Congratulations! You're starting to get to the big leagues. But when you do get there, I want you to make sure that you are the one monitoring the brand. No one will look after it like you can. You were the one to get the company and the brand to this point in its life, and no one has lived and breathed it the way you have. You are the one who should manage your brand and the direction it takes—not your advertising agency. I strongly recommend a book called ***Radical Marketing*** by Sam Hill and Glenn Rifkin. It tells you who should be the person running the marketing and branding of your company. As for tactics, look at the marketplace with your agency; assess what steps you want to take, and put a plan in place to achieve your goals. ***Remember to act like you are still a small company.*** If you don't, another small company will begin taking your brand share away, just like you once did!

7. Write a set of brand guidelines.

When you have created your brand name, its image will be accompanied by words and visuals that carefully position the brand to its target audience. It's time to make sure that you have a complete set of brand guidelines that can be followed easily and adhered to by anyone involved in promoting or selling your brand. These guidelines are not easy to create. Think about how many different pieces you have that carry your brand name. Use the brand concept overview for a list of all the items that might carry your logo and creative message. Your written guidelines must be clear and concise, covering every area that reflects your brand and its image, as well as every piece of communication. The instructions should be easily understandable and memorable by anyone using them. I realize that you may not have everything on the Total Branding list at this time, but it's never too early to get the guidelines started. Because someday, someone will need to get something done and you may not be there to oversee it, but all they'll have to do is refer to the guidelines.

8. Appoint a guardian of the brand.

One of the most important elements of growing your brand is the appointment of one person in your organization to be the brand's guardian. I'm going to repeat this: Appoint one person in your organization to be the guardian of the brand. The reasons for this are fairly obvious: Very careful control must be administered over the brand's impression and consistency. You have all played "telephone," where a few people sit in a circle and the first person whispers something into the ear of the second, the second whispers it into the ear of the third, and so on around the circle. By the time it ends at the last person, the phrase bears no resemblance to what it was when it started. **Don't let this happen to your brand's message.** Unfortunately, your message will get diluted and altered by the many people who handle it if you don't appoint a guardian. That person must have the final word and absolute control so that compliance and consistency can be ensured. The person should check on everything at the beginning, on any new items or new directions being proposed, and then on an as-needed basis.

Having run my own agency for many years and being in the advertising business my entire career, and working alongside the biggest agencies in the world, I can tell you that the very people you hire to help get out your message are often not working from your script. Pitching for a new account is part of running an agency; in fact, the larger agencies employ people who specialize in making new account pitches. What do you think a new agency or public relations firm will want to do if it wins your account? You've got it—it'll want to change your brand image. **Your gatekeeper must not let it.** You are the only one who has lived and breathed your brand. You created it! Don't let anyone change it. It's consistency over the long haul that really counts. It doesn't matter what your brand name is; it's what it represents that's important. If *you* don't think and act like a big boy, you will never be one.

9. Make your logo easy to read.

Be very careful about the shape and size of your logo and the accompanying type. Keep in mind that it will be used in all sorts of situations, so it must be legible to all age groups. For instance, the fact is that most people's eyesight begins to fail at around 45, so think about things like that in the developmental stage. Your logo not only must be impactive, but it must also be readable by your target audience.

Make sure that your logo fits into a horizontal format rather than a vertical one. A vertical logo may break the clutter, but it is very hard to work with across a broad range of communication pieces. Also, as the English language is read from left to right, so should your logo. Make it memorable so that it creatively reinforces your product and its positioning. Your logo is created not only to look good, but it's there to get your message across.

As I mentioned earlier, it is important to prepare a written brief for the creative group or agency that will be developing your logo. The brief should give specific words that must be included and a general idea of what message the logo should convey; a very definite mood and tone that it should impart; and a sampling of the competitive set. Don't leave these decisions to people who know less about your brand than you do! Here's an interesting aside: Although our company was called Sims Freeman O'Brien, clients always found a way of changing the name to meet their particular needs. One particular day I was standing in the reception of General Foods, talking to one of our client brand managers. He had to send something to our company, and he said, "I'll send it over to Sims this afternoon." This happened often, but it really is a peculiar feeling when your name is not being used in the conversation but it's you being talking about. A more famous version of how customers get things changed is the Federal Express story: It was the brand leader in its category for years, but discovered in its research that consumers were always calling the brand FedEx. It listened, and you now know the results.

10. Stick with your advertising. You'll get tired of it before 10% of your customers have seen it.

Keep consistent the overall message of your advertising, public relations, and promotional campaigns. This cannot be emphasized enough—consistency is vital to the success of your brand's growth. Periodically get all of your communications pieces—from letterhead to advertising and everything in between—and put them up on a wall, then stand back and ask yourself: Do these pieces all come from the same family?

Once you've developed an advertising image and message, **stick with it.** Don't let anyone change it. I promise you that most of your target audience will not yet have seen your message or your advertising. In fact, most companies and their ad agencies change direction before even 10% of the target audience have seen the ads run. Why? **They** tire of it, since they've seen it all day, every day. To you and them, it's so familiar; you begin to think everyone has seen it and must be as bored with it as you are. But don't change just because you're ready for a chance. Most of your potential customers haven't seen it once yet! Believe me!

11. Make a claim you can own.

When you're developing your message about your brand, state a claim that you can really justify. Sometimes that's not easy to do. But if you really think hard and long, you'll come up with something real and relevant about your product that you can own as yours. One of the brands I worked on was a national brand of dental floss, which is basically a piece of string. In fact, all of the brands are the same. Some of them have a coating on them, but it's essentially only the brand name that makes one better than the next. We used the copy line "Nobody makes a better dental floss." It gave the brand the chance to make the claim first and at the same time look like a brand leader in the marketplace. The reality was that nobody made a better dental floss, but no one made a worse one either. Nevertheless, the statement was correct, and it positioned itself as a brand leader. The facts are that the brand ended up gaining a whopping share gain—up to a new level, 49%.

When you are making a claim or statement about your product, simply ask yourself, "Can my competitors say this about their product too?" If they can, then try to walk away from the concept. If possible, it really should be something that only you can say or want to say about your company or product, or be a statement that you have registered and protected. In the exchange of trust between you and your potential customer, this claim is what you are offering them.

12. If you are #1, then say so!

Americans love a winner. We don't care who finished second or third. It's the way we're raised. We've all heard the expression "Second place is for losers." (With my marketing hat on, I'd argue that point, but that's another discussion.) If you have a product that's #1 in the U.S., #1 in Texas, #1 in Saddle River, New Jersey, or #1-nominated by your customers, any #1 claim should be leveraged to the max. Act like a winner, and say so if you are.

13. Sell quality.

Price is always a factor, regardless of what you make or produce. Someone will always make a cheaper version. It's easy to cut price and make it your point of difference. But let me tell you, it's a tough road to haul, and over time it will be a very difficult way to make consistent profits and increase sales. There is a range of pricing that is acceptable in your category; I urge you to make sure brand sells in the upper levels of pricing.

Pricing is made up of 2 parts. **The first is: What are customers prepared to pay for your brand? The second part is: What are customers prepared to pay for your brand? Sell quality.** If all things are equal, consumers will always choose the product with a quality image and recognizable brand name. People usually value a product directly in proportion to what they pay for it, and perceived quality is the difference between what the customer expects and what they actually get. Many years ago we were pitching for the Morsels account at Nestlé, and one of the big worries of the client was that we had not completed any food photography for them before. We had done a lot for other people but not for them, and the client was concerned, quite rightly, and reluctant to give us the business. We had to make sure that we quashed these fears in order to get their business, so we offered the following proposition: If they gave us the work, we would promise that they would be delighted with it. And if for any reason there were problems, we would redo it until they were satisfied. Even better, we said that if at any time they were not completely happy with the work, we would be willing to pay for their normal photographic studio to reshoot. This proposal was a real win-win concept—we did get the account, and the client just could not lose. And we won because we knew that we would do a great job, our product was good, and we were very confident about what the results would be.

14. Use borrowed equity wisely.

Sometimes in the life of your company and its brand, you will want to develop programs that put you in joint events with another manufacturer or service. This is known as a "borrowed equity" program or promotion. In today's marketplace it probably is one of the tools that you will be using more than you would ever have in the past; it really is a good way to get more coverage for your brand, at greatly reduced costs. The key is to make sure that the borrowed equity you are getting from your promotional partner gives credibility to your brand and, if possible, supports its position. For British Airways, one of our clients, we would always take the position of never initiating price reductions. But we would give added value when it was supportive of our brand's image. We developed many programs for British Airways and always made sure that the partner in the program matched or exceeded the image of the "world's favorite airline." If customers wanted to go to the theater, we would make sure that we block-booked the best seats in London's famous West End theatre district. If customers wanted to play golf, they could tee up at the one and only St. Andrews in Scotland, the home of golf; shopping at Harrods or Burberry, among others—all of these partners reflect the quality that British Airways wants for its brand. In a nutshell, make sure that your advertising or promotional partner has the same standards and values that your brand has. Try to get together with a brand or image that is clearly seen to have much more brand awareness than your brand, thus increasing the equity you are borrowing.

Here's how you create a winning borrowed equity program. First, select 5 or 6 of the categories that you feel are the best fit for your brands and then go 4- deep each in those categories. Next, create a generic promotional program for each category and produce visual pieces that will get the program across. Then a most important part: The proposal to the other potential partner should come from the president of your company and be directed to the other company's president. In my experience, the proposals that come from agencies, marketing people, or brand people just don't get the attention that a letter and package from and to the president of each company gets. Once you have managed to get a tie-in program established, make sure that you get an agreement from the partner that, for the next foreseeable future, if you want to conduct programs with a partner in their category it will be with them. This accomplishes 3 things: It gives a commitment that you are serious; it makes it a lot easier to get next year's version completed; and it keeps your competition from getting a chance to produce a borrowed equity program with your new partner.

15. Monitor your brand.

You've established your brand, and your "guardian of the brand" is keeping consistency in its messages. Your ad agency is being challenged but kept in check. You've put considerable time, effort, and money into developing the brand. You've been thinking and selling quality. Now what? **Check the marketplace for the level of awareness of your brand** regarding quality, loyalty, and customer satisfaction. Today there are many ways you can do this: a mall intercept, a focus group, an online group who buys your category. But most importantly, I recommend that you check whether your image is consistent and that your target audience is getting the impression you are striving for. Please do not live in isolation—check your customers, they will tell you if you are on track!

16. Spend an inordinate amount of time with your customers.

Don't stay in your office to make decisions about your brand. Ask your customers what they think! Spend time asking them questions, and take action based on their answers. You will learn more about the customer's image of your brand by conducting this kind of informal research on a regular basis than by any other method.

Think every day about your customers—who they are, where they live, what they do outside of work, what motivates them, anything that will enable you to get inside their heads and make them say "WOW" about your brand. Get out of the office and go see them. Let them know you're interested in them. They are the people who matter most. Theirs are the only opinions that really count. They buy your brand.

CHAPTER 7

CRM: IT'S THE CUSTOMERS, STUPID!

This chapter discusses Customer Relationship Management, a subject close to my heart. It will show you how to build the kind of relationships and partnerships that will enable you to keep customers for life.

The best way to build a successful business is through a transfer of trust between you and your customer, and one way to do that is by earning their business by being a really good supplier.

You build a business by building relationships where it becomes mutually beneficial to do business with one another. I do not think that "managing customers" is the right approach. I therefore developed my own version of what CRM really means, and it's something I hope you will take from this book:

CUSTOMERS REALLY MATTER.

While CRM is often looked at independently from most other communication vehicles that are used, I truly believe that it is actually just one more tool in the branding arsenal, and it is an area of business that must be installed if you want to make a difference.

Customer relationship management has been around as industry buzz words for many years. There have been volumes written about the subject, and in my opinion, it has become more complex than it needs to be. I have read an awful lot on the subject, and the more I read, the more confusing it gets. Recently I went onto a Web site that claims to be an authority on CRM; one of the areas it suggests you click on is the icon "What is

CRM." Guess how many explanations there were? Twelve! Twelve different experts, each with their own version of CRM. No wonder it seems complicated. So after reading all of those experts, I would like to offer you what I believe is the best description I have read on CRM:

"CRM extends the concept of selling from a discrete act performed by a salesperson to a continual process involving every person in the company. It is the art/science of gathering and using information about your customers to build customer loyalty and increase customer value. With the current state of information technology, and high customer service expectations, it's practically impossible to consider these process issues without addressing technology, but it's important to remember that customer relationships—human relationships—are the ultimate driving force." Larry Tuck, **Sales and Marketing Management** magazine

To sum it up, whatever else anyone tells you or whatever you read—remember this, CUSTOMERS REALLY MATTER. If you get involved in a CRM program, it can be all-encompassing, and it can become incredibly expensive to install if you let it, but I believe that you can also become selective in its use. In this case I believe that it is one time that you can be a little bit pregnant. I have used the concept over the years in clients' companies and my own; it really does make a difference in the way we work, the way our workmates think about our companies, and the way our customers think about our products and us. And guess what? It will make a positive impact on the bottom line over the long haul! I hope that this chapter will give you a good feeling for what you can accomplish by implementing some or all of the ideas mentioned and that you will be inspired to take further steps on incorporating CRM in your business. I would suggest that you read up on the subject, since there are plenty of books out there, but make sure to not forget: CUSTOMERS REALLY MATTER. (By the way, even if you don't put in a Customer Relationship Management program immediately, at least focus on the Customer Relationship part; the Management part can come later.)

As I have mentioned before, if you do not believe in running a customer-centric organization, then you probably will not be successful in incorporating a CRM initiative in your company. I would suggest that you install an incentive program that is measured by customer satisfaction if you want to get the maximum return out of it. There are plenty of places where you can learn more about CRM than you probably ever want to know. Beware—because much of the information is driven by manufacturers of the systems that they are trying to sell you something. There are many suppliers and consultants out there who are delighted to help you in your CRM journey. Each one has a different approach to looking at CRM; therefore, I would take the time to look them over, after establishing what you and your team think are the company's requirements. There are many CRM packages available, but in all honesty, not all are right for you, and not one company has everything that you need. Spend a good amount of time making sure that the results you want from your CRM program are in sync with the overall marketing strategy of the company. I would strongly suggest that you emphasize researching companies of your size that have installed CRM programs successfully; speak to the people who use the systems and, if possible, some of their customers.

Just for the record, CRM is not something new—good companies and good leaders have known for eons that you have to look after your customers, and your best customers most. And as I said in the beginning of this section, you can be a little bit pregnant; it's not just for major corporations. Even if you are a one-man company, you should still give serious thought to installing some of the CRM initiatives.

A good friend of mine, Richard Gerson—who runs a really successful company based in Tampa, Florida, that specializes in CRM—wrote an article titled "Secrets of CRM Success." It included these 4 P's of CRM, which I think really encapsulate what the real ingredients of a successful CRM initiative are.

THE 4 P'S OF CRM

PLANNING: Develop a plan of what you want to accomplish in the short term and in 3 to 5 years. If you don't know where you are going, you can't get there. You don't want to buy the wrong technology for the data you want to capture.

PEOPLE: Make sure your partners and employees are on board. They must all be supportive and be team players. Train them to be a customer-centric company. They are the people doing the day-to-day customer interaction.

PROCESS: Take the time to identify your CRM process; these are the steps of how your customer contracts your company, how you process the information that you receive, and then how you use this information to revisit the customer repeatedly.

PLATFORM: This is the technology you're going to use. Spend the right amount of time to find the software and Web integration that works for you and for your customers. Ask people who have experienced the installation and use of CRM in their companies.

By the way, CRM isn't foolproof. General Motors had implemented a CRM system that decided what vehicles to push off the lots. At the same time the data was being collected, another General Motors group had put in a promotion to get rid of some very ugly lime-green cars, so the sale of those cars skewed the data. They cranked up the line to produce even more ugly green cars!

Installing a CRM concept is not always easy. Sometimes things can go wrong, and from my experience, it's usually because we think that a computer program will do the job for us—it won't. If you have decided to make the company a customer-centric organization, you absolutely have to ensure that all in the management team are on board with the concept and that it trickles down to the rest of the organization. The other point that confuses a lot of companies is that they think CRM is basically a data-based marketing program; well, it can be, but that is only one part of a *successful* Customers Really Matter program.

On the 4th of July in 1976 a couple of monumental events occurred for me. It was, of course, the bicentennial of the independence of the United States. I remember exactly where I was. It was the New York harbor—tall ships; red white, and blue everything! Also, it happened to be the day I started my company in America. In my mind, the opening of my company was the more important—what a thrill as an immigrant to America. I remember starting my business and thinking, **OK, I have got everything in place to get started.** I had seen my lawyers and accountants, visited the bank, prepared all of my letterheads and stationery, started looking at where I was going and developing my marketing plan, etc. Had the phone switched on, bought a car, a handheld calculator (pretty hip in those days), and had a couple of chairs and a desk put into the apartment's second bedroom. Now I was in business—I was on my way. I was full of myself, in a quite naïve way, and I really felt quite good until it occurred to me: *I don't have any customers.* It just hit me like a ton of bricks.

The one thing I needed more than anything else at that moment was a customer. It didn't matter how good my company brochure looked, and it didn't matter what my business cards said if I didn't have customers to give them to! This is the basis of what we are about to get into: how you can build a relationship with your customers that will enable you to keep them, if you want to, for life. I want you to build your businesses on the basis of earning the customers you get—that is, you get good customers by being a good supplier or manufacturer. You get to keep them by making sure that you have built a relationship to last through ups and downs, by having customers transfer their trust to you. It takes a lot of real work to get that trust, so treat it like a pair of kid gloves.

Hopefully, you will have and keep your customers for years. But no matter how much you try, at some point you will lose a customer, and the facts are that it takes about 7 times as much time, effort, and money to get a new customer as it would to retain the old one. And here's another interesting statistic: For every customer who complains about you or your company, there are probably 8 to 10 people who didn't tell you their feelings. So whatever you do, please make sure that you have an ongoing dialogue with your customer base, just so that you can know what their feelings are and what action you may have to take, good or bad. CUSTOMERS FIRST. That should be your mantra; if you only get one thing from this section, that's it—CUSTOMERS FIRST. There are many things that can help you to be successful in business, but the one thing you simply cannot do without are your customers.

Here are the first steps that I would like you to consider in growing your customer numbers and developing the relationships that will positively affect the bottom line.

Step 1. Produce a list of all of your customers and rank them in order of sales, the largest customer ranking at #1 down to the smallest. This is your customer base. That's easy enough! There are plenty of computer programs that you can use to format this into a visual impression of this customer base. I think of it like a stack of customers.

Step 2. I would like you to segment these customers into 4 groups or blocks: A, B, C, and D. Naturally, your A customers are your best ones, the customers who buy from you most frequently. They are your best customers, and they spend more money with you than any other group. This is your strength, the backbone, the single most important group of customers.

You can decide on the units that you use to divide the groups: It can be a dollar amount, units, returns; it really doesn't matter, as long as it is relevant to your business.

Just the fact that you are dividing the customers into 4 groups will tell you that they are not equal—wouldn't you want to have all of your customers in the A group? Well, that's what CRM is about: trying to make all of your customers into A's.

Like we said in an earlier chapter on your customers, we have to decide on the LCD, the lowest common denominator. There is no big surprise here; your customers probably have a lot in common with each other. It is a good idea to write down the details that you think go into making your ideal customers. Build a profile or what an A customer's attributes are; you probably know them really well, you likely are like-minded when you are with them, and it's a good bet this is not by accident. In a subconscious way you already know what the customers likes and dislikes, so you adjust the way you interact with them accordingly. You may talk to them about their families; go to the ball game with them, have lunches, give them articles from magazines that you think might be relevant, and on and on. You probably consider them friends as well as business associates. Therefore, if you could write down what you think makes an A customer, wouldn't it be easier for a new sales employee, or even you, to be able to focus on the targets that you want to become A customers? This, then, is the A Customer Profile. Obviously, we can't get them all to become A customers, but let's at least try to get them to be our B customers, on through C and D customers.

OK, so that's fairly easy so far. Now I would like you to think about extending the depth of the building blocks. Imagine putting 3 more blocks under the D block to build your business. Block E will be for ex-customers. Next is Block F, future customers—up-and-coming potential patrons who you have identified as a group. They may well fit into one or all 4 of the building blocks A, B, C, or D. But make no mistake about it, you should put the maximum amount of effort into getting new customers who will go into the A block first—or certainly go after customers that have the best potential to become A customers. And block G is for the customers that I call the "greater majority": the balance of the category that your products are marketed in.

So let's define our 4 basic blocks:

Block A customers: Your largest customers in terms of sales, they buy more frequently than any other group, and they will have bought from you more than any of the other groups. You probably have an intimate working relationship with all of the customers in this block—they are your friends and your best customers. Wouldn't you like all your customers to be just like these? Usually this block of customers will represent about 1% to 2% of your total customers. It will vary, but usually it's around those numbers.

Block B customers: Those in this group buy products regularly from you but maybe not as frequently as the A block. Their purchases are not quite as large, but some may have the potential to become A customers with some extra effort and attention. You probably have the knowledge and information you need that will enable you to move them up to the A block. These are people to whom you can demonstrate a real difference by helping them grow their companies, as opposed to just trying to sell them more! This block will usually represent about 4% to 5% of your customer base.

Block C customers: This is a mixed group; they may be new or have been with your company for a long time. They may be just jogging along, making no real move toward becoming B customers, but nevertheless good clients. There are a heck of a lot of them, probably amounting to around 15% of your customer base. They are really good solid customers but just really do not deliver the highest level of sales and profits. But as I said, there are a lot of them, and that makes them an important group.

Block D customers: This is the largest group of your customer base, representing around 80% of the total. They do only a small amount of business with you at this time, or even may be only embryonic customers, and they take a great deal of time, effort, money, and resources to serve. However, they are still customers. This block has to be handled in a very special way, and we may have to make some hard decisions about them. You have to find out what their upside potential is? Do you want them to stay? Will they stay? What will it take? Do they have the potential to get to become C, B, or even A customers?

Now we should compare each building block's proportional profit. In most companies, profit is a bulked-up number, meaning that the normal procedure is to add all of the sales numbers up, work out a gross profit number, and then take out all cost of doing business, which results in a net profit number. The problem with this is that the real costs are not correctly allocated, as they should be, against individual customers. This is an area that you can work with your controller, accounts department, or accounting company. And by using a customer-based accounting technique, you will get factual information of how your customers are performing.

THE SAD THING IS THAT YOU MAY HAVE TO "FIRE" SOME CUSTOMERS. If your company is anywhere near normal, the numbers will probably shock you: The top 20% of your customers will probably show more than 100% of your profits. That's not possible, right?

Actually, it is, if you treat each customer with the correct apportioned amount of overhead (accounting costs, collections, sales rep time, advertising and marketing, etc.). It will probably show you that a lot of your customers are actually costing you money to do business with them. So again, YOU MAY HAVE TO FIRE SOME CUSTOMERS.

One of the fringe benefits of going through this exercise is that it will clearly show you that around 70% of your management dollars are spent on blocks B, C, and D but only 30% against our existing businesses. While I am a huge advocate of getting the corporate message across to as many customers as possible, the concept of looking at the return on investment by the different groups will certainly get you to think differently.

So now that we have all of this information, what the heck are we going to do with it? Should we "FIRE ALL OF OUR D CUSTOMERS"—we are losing money on them, right? No, of course not—they do help us with some economies of scale, and some of them may well have the potential of becoming C customers. Or they may well be A customers of your competitors, and wouldn't you want them to be your A customer? What you should do is produce an analysis and a profile of each and every D customer to determine what the upside potential is. Then, and only then, decide if you should continue doing business with that particular company.

Now, what does all this mean? Well, the objective is to move customers up the building blocks. Let's go back to the blocks we have already built. Remember, over a period of time, you will always lose some customers: Some of the E (ex-) customers will come back, some F's (future customers) will become D or even C customers, and possibly some G's (the greater majority) will come into the fold.

However, if you can move only 1% of your total accounts or customers up the building blocks, you will see an increase to the top and bottom line that far exceeds the time effort and money it would take to get new business added up to the same numbers. All I am asking is that you move 1% of your customers up the building blocks. The results are simply incredible! You can look for performance improvement of around 15% to the bottom line, for only a top-line improvement of over 6%. That's a lot of profit for very little increase in sales, don't you think?

What's the net of it all? 1. Look after the customers you have. 2. Go get the new customers that you have identified that have A potential. 3. Try to persuade all of your customers to buy more. I know this sounds easy, but Customers are what Customer Relationship Management is all about.

Let's move on to another area: Marketing budgets and allocations. We all want new customers, don't we? That's perfectly normal, and most companies feel the same way, and so do the marketing and salespeople who help you go to market with your products. It's much more fun! The downside is that it takes a lot more time, money, and effort to get a **new** customer. It costs about 7 times the amount of money to get a new customer than it does to look after one you have, due to more advertising, more sales calls, more introductory pricing, more management time, etc. In fact, the averages of monies spent will probably shock you. If you look at your marketing dollars spent, you will probably see that up to 60–80% are aimed at non-customers. As a marketing guy, I will fight with myself over this one, but the facts are what they are. I would like to repeat that you should seriously think about the way you spend your advertising and marketing dollars. Use them where they get the most benefit—your existing customers, and if you can reach your A customers more than the others, then even better.

Are your customers happy with you? Do you know what they really think about you and your services? You should. The real thinking behind the building block concept is to use a "ladder" and make them upwardly mobile. Satisfied is just not good enough—I want your customers to say, "WOW, they are a great company that always comes through and delivers more than I ever expected." The objective is to get your customers to move up from one building block to the next—it's that simple. If your customers are less than thrilled with your companies' products and/or services, then your competition will convert them. Make your existing customer base your top priority; treat it with kid gloves. Again, your mantra should be CUSTOMERS FIRST. Of course, you cannot expect every customer to move up, since some will always be quite happy staying where they are, but the objective is to move as many customers upward as is realistically possible.

All customers are not equal: Another benefit of a CRM program is that it will make you think about, and put a value on, the "lifetime value" of your customers. How often have you thought about this? You have heard the saying that all customers are equal! That's just not the case—some customers are far more equal than others. What you have to do is estimate the average lifetime that your customers stay with your company—this will, of course, vary by category. Let's assume that your customers stay the normal average of 7 years, and if your A customers spend $100,000 per annum, your B customers spend $60,000 per annum, your C's spend $20,000, and your D's spend $2,000. When you add up all the numbers, the seven-year values of the groups are:

A's	$700,000
B's	$420,000
C's	$140,000
D's	$14,000

If this doesn't illustrate the point that not all customers are equal, I have more evidence: Cadillac in its research has shown that its best customers have a lifetime value of around $350,000 to $400,000. But the one to shock me was that Taco Bell's customers are worth a lifetime value of $18,000. That's a lot of tacos, and I know that I'm not included in the numbers, so someone is buying an awful lot!

By getting a lifetime value of your customers, then you can make an informed decision on what direction you want to go. A big part of the upward migration of customers into higher building blocks relates to making sure that the customers are valuable to you. They should deliver a margin that makes them a customer that is worth keeping, or at least worth giving your time and attention to.

You should also make sure that you are building the relationship with your customers that hopefully will enable you to remain "partners in business" for a lifetime, especially if you are in a 2-step distribution category. Make sure that you work with these customers to help them grow their businesses. Help them create programs that will drive traffic to their outlets—and not always specifically to buy your products. You have got to want your customers to grow, make more money, and buy more from you!

Being "customer-focused" means everyone in the company, from the president to the delivery person, the receptionist to the accounting department. You have to lead by example—show how you walk the walk. Also, make sure that you have set aside time and money for your staff to make sure that they really understand and are able to invoke a customer-focused organization. There is a well-known book called **Don't Sweat the Small Stuff**—well, I just don't agree. You really should sweat the small stuff, for it's those little details that will impress your customers. Make sure that everyone in your organization clearly understands that "customer-focused" is not an idea that management has just thought of. They all must clearly understand that this is the way we will go about business.

Are your customers satisfied? If you answered yes to this question you answered it wrong. The prerequisite for your company should be to try to get as many of your customers from "satisfied" to the "really satisfied." Your customers that are just "satisfied" are very susceptible to competitive activities, so they must be persuaded to feel even more positive about your company. Make this a priority. How will you know if you are running an organization or even a department in which the customers are highly satisfied? You won't unless you ask them questions. Find out from your customers if they are happy with your company, its level of service, quality of product, attitude of employees, etc. This is how you can get your customers to move up the building blocks.

Once you have prepared the questions about your performance level, how should you use them? To reiterate, you don't have to treat all of your customers the same. For instance, your A customers should get personal interviews with the management team; certain A customers should meet with the president of the company and go through the questionnaire. The B customers should get interviews from the sales and marketing staff. The C customers should get at least phone interviews. And finally, the D customers should get the questionnaire faxed or e-mailed. Be realistic: You simply cannot have your top people trying to speak to every customer—it just won't get done. This process is critical to helping you go forward with your business; it will not happen perfectly, but be patient and make sure you get as much participation across the board as you possibly can.

OK, so now we have all of the information about our customers and are now in a position to do something with it. First, by looking at the results of the questions, you will be able to determine exactly where to put your energies into making improvements and leveraging the good things that are also going on.

One of the main controls and tools that you should invoke is to produce a much more complete customer profile sheet. It should have all of the basic information on the customer (plus, of course, whatever is current in sales terms, any problems, what's being produced, etc.)—in fact, everything that is relevant to this particular customer—so that anyone in the company who might be communicating with him or her will have every piece of current and historic information available. The customer profile sheet should be updated every time there is contact, and be available to all members of the company. The results will be that everyone will have a role in making the customer a priority. In other words, CUSTOMERS FIRST.

Nobody really likes change, and implementing putting a new program will probably not sit well with your employees initially. One of the best ways to ensure participation and enthusiasm is to put some sort of incentive scheme in place to reward them for whatever level of increase you are seeking. I would strongly suggest that you make very clear what your expectations are from them by confirming with them the program's objectives. They should also reinforce what they see to be their job functions under the new CRM initiative. Hopefully, this new direction will include how they see their roles as helping themselves to grow, how it will benefit the company, and—last but certainly not least—how will they be helping the customer. Then clarify with your employees what you see their roles are, and tell them that they will be measured against specific criteria—people always perform better when they are being measured. The actual criteria being measured will vary from company to company, but of course, they could be as simple as sales dollars increased, percentage increase, units shipped this month, reduction of complaints, on-time deliveries—as many as you can think of. But you must put a reward system in place that will benefit all employees who participate if they do achieve their goals. This really is a win-win situation: They will want to succeed, and when they do, then you do too!

How can you make the sales department more effective? There are many ways to do this, and as this is a book on branding, I will not spend a great deal of time on the subject. (Frankly, there are many more qualified people than I.) As you will have gathered by now, A customers are far more valuable than your B's, and so on. So we need to make sure that your salespeople are now spending the appropriate amount of time to each of the target building blocks. For instance, we know that each salesperson has approximately 250 days a year to interact with customers (50 work weeks X 5 days = 250 days), so how can we make these days more effective? What I would like you to do is make a matrix—basically, this will compute the amount of visits you feel your customers should get from your salespeople in a year. This could be once a year if they have 250 A customers—highly unlikely, but if they do, then you are making a lot of money. More realistically, they will probably have about 5 A customers, and you should decide that they should be seen, let's say, at least once a month. This will give them a total of 60 days a year that the salesperson should be spending with them.

Assuming they each have around 20 B customers, they will see them once a quarter, which equals 80 days. The 75 C customers will get a once-a-year visit. Including A customer visits, this totals 215 sales days in front of the customers. Now the salespeople still have 35 days left to attend to other functions, seminars, training, trade fairs, grandmother's funeral, etc. But the most important part is that they now will have an agenda that they must keep, and they are able to make their whole year's calendar in advance. They also have a measurement put in place to ensure that they do complete the visits, and on a timely basis. This really is a great tool to ensure that they spend the correct amount of time with the right people, your customers. And as a side note, by putting a program like this in place, it accomplishes 2 goals: It really cements the relationships between customers and the company, and it reduces the risks that can occur when a vital member of the team leaves—because the person who takes over the territory will already have the appointments to visit the customers.

While preparing the dates of these meetings, you should also get a matrix of what other promotional support is being given to the A's, B's, C's, and D's. Let's assume that they will get advertising support, co-op dollars, P.R., outdoor media, trade shows, mailings, promotions, and all of the other media. But now you should prepare a marketing plan for each and every dealer (if you have a 2-step distribution product), who will include all of the sales objectives that you have established for this customer. The team should establish these sales goals, because if it is responsible for presenting them to you, then it is also responsible for producing them too. Also, you will list all of the support you will give the team to achieve these goals. Ideally, the customer support will vary in its level on a graduated scale, A through D. This marketing plan should be agreed to by the customers (dealer) and signed off on by them and the salesperson; they both have to commit to the expected territory sales numbers. Now you have a measuring tool to go back and talk to the customer on a regular basis and also to make sure that your company is at the fore of his mind. If sales are down, obviously you want to be able to find out why quickly, then you can do something about it.

So if you look after your best customers and try to improve the quality of business with the rest, you will see a dramatic difference in the bottom line without a dramatic increase in effort. **CUSTOMERS REALLY MATTER.**

CHAPTER 8

THINK LIKE A CUSTOMER

I hope the previous chapter managed to convince you that focusing on your customer will make a dramatic difference to your relationships and improve the bottom line for the long term. However, there are other philosophies that will also improve the performance of your brand. One is: **Think like a customer.**

When Bill Clinton was running for office he had the support and assistance of James Carville as his campaign manager. James figured out early on in the campaign that it was all about the economy, and for the duration of the campaign he kept a sign on his desk that read, "It's the economy, stupid." I am sure that focusing on the economy really was one of the major factors in getting President Clinton elected. I would like you to be as focused on your customers as James was on the economy—maybe even make a sign for your desk that reads, **"It's the customers, stupid."**

Business has changed dramatically in the last few years—it's just not as simple as putting out a lot of advertising on TV, radio, and print. Broad-based marketing certainly has its place, and I am a staunch supporter of the traditional media. But it's the way that we go to business that we might want to revisit. If you were going to start your brand from scratch again, would it look like it does today? Chances are that it would not!

Therefore, I would suggest that an exercise worth doing is to play "What If": What if we did start again? What would the customer experience be like?

The first question should be: "If I were a customer of my brand, what would be the things that I would want, and how would I like to be treated?

Just suppose you are in the market for a new piece of furniture: How would you feel if you were offered our new couch or seating group in not 3 months but 3 weeks?

A new car in 3 days; a new, custom-made suite in 24 hours (just like they do in Hong Kong)?

Why not get paid on an insurance claim in 24 hours?

For instance, we all travel a lot and have experienced trains, planes, automobiles, hotels, car rentals, travel agents, and all of the other "moving experiences." Are you satisfied with all of these experiences? I hope not! The airlines have been going through some tough times over the last few years—their stock prices have fallen, fuel costs have risen, and they have lots of reasons to not make a profit. Hotels have suffered the same fate, but the one area that they do control is the customer experience, yet most are just not getting the job done. Let's play "What If" with the hotel experience.

Today, you can go online to get your reservations estimated and confirmed, but how nice would it be if you were actually offered the lowest rate available instead of having to pry it out of the person at the other end of the line? Imagine that the person had a profile of you (not actually you, but their ideal customer profile, that probably looks like you) even though you had not stayed at that particular hotel before, only the chain that they belonged to. But if you had stayed at their chain before, they would automatically know or would have asked you the type of room you like, what floors you liked or didn't like, and the teas and sodas you preferred. Now, as you are a repeat customer (to the chain) and maybe even that particular hotel, they will do everything possible to make sure that you get a room upgrade. The fact that they are trying to get you an upgrade will be communicated to you, and while it may not be available, at least you know that they are aware of your unique status and will do everything to make sure that you are recognized in some way. Wouldn't it be nice if your car was automatically valet parked when you arrived to check in and was retrieved as many times as you wanted it, always with a smile?

Maybe they even offer to clean it for FREE if you are staying for 2 nights or more. How many times have you arrived at a hotel destination to be told that check-in doesn't start until 3 p.m.? This really hits home if you have flown in the "red eye" from L.A. to the East Coast. Wouldn't it be special if you were told that as a repeat chain customer you can check in anytime you want! Then when you got to the room, there were candles burning as well as some fresh-cut flowers to welcome you, because your profile said so. They know that you were a traveling business person and you need to look good, so they automatically offer to press your suit, and every night your shoes were taken, shined, and returned by 6 a.m. through a flap in the door. (When I was a kid in Europe, they used to do this.) Because you use the room for bringing clients, you are able to get the room cleaned at whatever specific time you would like it.

We are all traveling with CDs or tapes of music; it would be thoughtful if they put in equipment to play them on, as well as providing a VCR and DVD player with a selection of movies that are available form the library. And because you have stayed with the chain before, they would give you a welcome gift that really is something you can use: maybe a haircut in their salon or theater tickets locally.

Most of these ideas are not expensive, just not enacted—these are really big opportunities for a hotel group to differentiate and separate itself from the competition.

Here's a true story relating to "thinking like a customer" that had a profound effect on me. Many years ago I was working at the London Hilton hotel. Before the opening, we worked in bedrooms—they were the only rooms that were ready, since the offices were not built yet. Three days before the opening I was working in the bedroom, and the chief engineer, George, came in and asked me if he could make a visual inspection of the room. I watched him check the room out; he had a clipboard and ticked off what seemed like a hundred items. He then said he wanted to check out the bathroom; I just tagged along to see what he would do. Again, he went through a checklist: taps, caulking, mirrors, wallpaper, etc. Then he did something that would change the way I thought about business for the remainder of my career: Fully clothed, he stepped into the bathtub and lay back. Shocked, I asked what the heck he was doing; his response was, "Jack, I am looking at the bathroom the way the customer will."

Wow! In my opinion, this is one of the best pieces of advice I can ever pass along—make sure that you run your business with the mind-set that your customers are the reason that you are in business. Grow your brand as a customer-centric operation; don't just pay lip service to this way of thinking. This customer-first strategy is very hard to make it become the way you do business, but it will make a positive difference for the long haul and certainly give you the edge over the competition.

Interestingly, when developing your promotional programs and executions with your trade buyers and/or the end consumer, one of the people you have to be very careful about is *you*— and your agencies, if you have them. You see, you don't think like your customers: You don't have the same wants or needs as your customers, and you probably have nothing in common with them. Therefore, when you or your agencies are developing promotional programs such as advertising, promotions, trade events, and the like, you must try to put yourself in the customers' positions. A number of years ago, Keith Reinhard, who was the head of DDB Worldwide—realized very clearly that the people who worked in his agencies around the world were not the customers of the brands they worked on. So he decided to conduct a poll of the general public and the people who worked in the agencies to see how far apart their attitudes and thinking really were. He called the research...

"I HAVE MET THE CUSTOMER, AND HE AIN'T ME"

The differences are incredible, and I hope it will reinforce the "Think Like a Customer" concept. Here is how the agency employees and the general public differed on just a few of the important issues they asked about:

1. Job security is more important than money.
   Agency: 52%   General public: 75%

2. My greatest achievements are still ahead of me.
   Agency: 89%   General public: 65%

3. Couples should live together before getting married.
   Agency: 50%   General public: 33%

4. TV is my primary form of entertainment.
   Agency: 28%   General public: 53%

5. My favorite type of music is classic rock.
   Agency: 64%   General public: 35%

You can clearly see that when marketers and agencies develop communication programs, they see the world through completely different eyes than the people they are trying to reach. Make sure you sit with your internal and external groups so that they absolutely get this before they start on any promotional program development. Make sure that you conduct some qualitative research—know your consumer. Make your company and your agencies **think like the customer,** and you will create far more effective advertising and promotional programs.

CHAPTER 9

CREATING A PROMOTION THAT WILL GROW YOUR BRAND!

Promotion is particularly dear to my heart: As you read earlier, our company was ranked as the #1 marketing and promotion agency in America for the 2 years before I retired. Throughout my career we created and produced many winning promotions that really moved the sales needle for our clients; some just get a little more recognition than others. One particular program I was particularly proud of was the really great job we did for our client Nestlé. It also happened to win the highest award given out in the promotional marketing industry, the "Super Reggie." Not only was the program a big win for us (and I have to single out Liz Lombardi as the account person that handled the Nestlé account for us), but it was also a big win for our client, who allowed us to create a program that really broke through the clutter to gain substantial sales. It was, however, a brand-building program that uses different tools and media to reach the target audience. The name of the winning program was...

WHO LAID A FINGER ON MY BUTTERFINGER?

We developed an all-inclusive marketing and promotional campaign to support the Nestle Butterfinger/Simpsons tie-in program. The program objectives were to get incremental sales from the youth market (12–24) and reinforce the brand's fun and mischievous personality.

We created a "whodunit" mystery program, with a grand prize of $50,000 in cash going to the lucky contestant who found out who the culprit was. Detective Bart Simpson was featured on 65 million Butterfinger bars as well as on special packaging in stores and vending machines nationwide.

Consumers played the game by collecting clues found inside the Butterfinger bar wrappers, then mailing in their solutions. The program was given a great deal of media support, including a 30-second TV spot and a radio campaign featured in the top 100 markets, where listeners called in to give what they thought was the answer. We gave prizes to 5 players in each market and a chance to play for a trip to a concert of their choice. Also, there were in-store materials and features in *TV Guide*. And 10,000 winners received T-shirts featuring Bart Simpson in his detective outfit.

What happened? Besides someone winning the grand prize, the brand had a sales gain of 51% during the promotional period and managed to get featured in 47 trade and consumer magazines.

This program was a winner for our client Nestlé, the trade, the consumers, and our company too!

I thought that it might be relevant to show you how we go through the developmental process in creating a promotional marketing program that you can follow in creating programs for your brand, so here it is:

PROMOTION DEVELOPMENT PROCESS

The Brief

Development of every program starts with a well-written brief. This document, whether written in a formal format or not, will provide background information about the product, the competition, market dynamics, and retail class of trade or account where the program will be executed. It will confirm the objectives for the promotion, the target audience, and what success will look like. The planning brief will establish a strategy against which all ideas will be evaluated.

The brief will help to assess whether a promotion is what's needed to address the current issues or opportunities and, if so, which promotional tactics should be considered.

I cannot emphasize enough how important it is to spend enough time on the creation of the brief. You must establish the reason why you want to promote, what the objectives are, and what measurements you will put in place to confirm whether it has been successful. Make sure that the promotion rationale in the brief has the blessing of all stakeholders before proceeding to idea generation.

Brainstorm Brief

For those intimately involved with the promotion, the more information, the better. For purposes of the brainstorm, however, an edited version of the brief should be distributed. This brief will focus on the product, the objectives, the target audience, the timing, past promotions that have worked, past promotions that have not worked, and any constraints and/or considerations.

This should provide brainstorm invitees with enough information to think without constricting the creative process.

Distribute the brief prior to the brainstorm to allow those who will be participating an opportunity to come with ideas.

The Brainstorm

The best brainstorms happen when people from different walks of life participate: e.g., account types from various account groups and "creatives" (people from the creative departments), as well as people within the target audience you're trying to reach—moms with kids ages 3 to 5, etc.
The brainstorm starts with a review of the brief.

A moderator is appointed to start the group thinking, keep the ideas flowing, and expand upon them, minimizing the private conversations among the group.

A second person should be appointed to record all the ideas generated.

The moderator often presents different topics to the group to get the discussion going, but once the group has started to participate, ideas should be allowed to flow without interruption. It's the moderator's job to encourage everyone in the group to participate and to move the group to a different topic once he/she feels the topic being discussed has been exhausted.

THERE ARE NO BAD IDEAS IN A BRAINSTORM!

Concept Development

Don't be concerned with arriving at "the big idea" at the brainstorm. It is usually necessary to have the notes transcribed and distributed to a smaller group, which will review and select those ideas that should be developed further. Remember: KEEP IT SIMPLE. The best promotions are those that are easy to understand and easy to participate in. If at first, you don't succeed...a second brainstorm is not usually necessary but always an option.

At this stage it is wise to "test" the concepts. This can be done in a variety of ways—e.g., a simple survey among office colleagues, a preview with key retailers, informal focus groups of people within the target audience, mall intercepts, etc., depending upon how much money is available. There are now companies like **Think 360** that can actually test promotions and give a good forecast on what will happen when it gets into the market.

Once testing is complete and all stakeholders agree on the promotion to be executed, you're ready to go.

Depending upon the idea developed, you may need to bring in outside vendors to execute, such as sweepstakes administrators, a fulfillment house, etc. If so, review the idea with each of these vendors—collectively, if possible, to work out any kinks.

The Creative Execution

The creative brief will provide your creative team with the specifics for all the elements needed to bring the promotion to life. It will include a description of "how it works": the tone and manner, the target audience, the advertising and POS elements available to communicate the promotion, creative mandates, logo placement, acceptable colors and production specifications. At this stage it is very important to make sure that the creative development is kept in sync with the overall image and creative that is being used for the rest of your creative communications, it must tie back to the "essence of the brand". The creative team should also be apprised of the deadline as well as the budget available for stock photography, illustration, photo shoot, etc. The creative team has to make sure that it is cognizant of the brand's overall creative direction—to ensure that it looks as though it belongs! This part of the communication process can easily go in a different direction than you intended, so you have to make sure that doesn't happen.

The creative team usually consists of a writer and art director to ensure a creative concept is developed equally by both disciplines. The creative team will be responsible for creative development, securing the illustrator and/or photographer, negotiating rights for any artwork, and coordinating with the production department and/or printer to ensure that all ideas are executable, within budget, and timing deadlines.

Creative communications should be reviewed periodically during its development to make sure it sticks to strategy and avoids any surprises at completion.

Final the creative concepts should be reviewed and approved by all internal stakeholders, the sweepstakes administrator, the fulfillment company, and legal and key accounts (if applicable) before being produced.

Production

Get yourself a good production manager or a printer you can trust! This is the phase in which the most problems can occur—and the most miracles can happen. The problems can be avoided by reviewing concepts with production during the development phase and reminding your production manager/printer (over and over again) of the budget and timing deadlines.

It's smart to be present when the job is on press—once again, to avoid any surprises after the job has been printed.

The Sell-in to the trade

All your hard work is in vain if you don't excite the sales force, who in turn must excite the retailer. This can be done in many ways, including creating a similarly themed "promotion" to help "sell-in" to the promotion to the trade.

"Themed" sales meetings, video broadcasts, and even well-designed, informative sales materials can do the trick.

Put some meat in the materials. Provide the sales force with a good story for the retailer—such as what this program will do to lift sales of the category as well as the product, or how similar programs in the past have increased traffic, sales, and profit. Know the hot buttons of your key accounts, and customize the story and the presentation to appeal to each of them.

Execution

Gone are the days when you can create a promotion, send it out in the field, and assume it will be executed correctly. Your only shot at flawless execution is to take control of the promotion yourself. If you cannot provide the resources, there are outside agencies that can check stores to make sure materials are there, product is stocked, and managers and employees are educated about the promotion.

Do your own spot checks. Visit the stores around you to try to participate as a consumer. Determine whether there are any flaws that should be corrected immediately. If so, fix them!

Evaluation

At the conclusion of the promotion, evaluate its effect on meeting the objectives established during the planning phase. Talk to retailers, talk to consumers, talk to those in customer service, those who fulfilled the offer. Get as much feedback as you can and revise the program accordingly. Many of the promotions considered "best in class" are repeated year after year after year. The key is to make it better each year.

APPENDICES
FORMS AND QUESTIONNAIRES

Brand to the Bone strength!

Complete the following questions and rank your brand, company product or service on a scale of 1–5, 1 being poor and 5 excellent. Give yourself 3 if you cannot answer the question. Total the answers to see how your brand ranks.

CORPORATE

1. Does the head of the company lead the branding direction? 1 2 3 4 5

2. Does everyone in your organization know what your brand stands for and is able to communicate it clearly to your customers? 1 2 3 4 5

3. Are you sure that all departments coordinate their branding efforts? 1 2 3 4 5

4. Do you check every department or service to make sure it delivers the brand impression you want to achieve?
    1 2 3 4 5

5. Do you get key employees to review and sign off on all of the communication pieces and programs that leave the company? 1 2 3 4 5

6. Do you train employees on how you want the brand to be represented? 1 2 3 4 5

7. In your internal meetings does someone represent the brand and customers point of view?
        1 2 3 4 5

8. Do you have an internal "Guardian of the Brand"?
    1 2 3 4 5

9. Do you have meetings to discuss the brand's strength and condition?
    1 2 3 4 5

10. If you have various products, does your corporate brand support them?
    1 2 3 4 5

11. Do your key employees get feed back on all of the customer input?
    1 2 3 4 5

12. Can the employees quote the company mission statement?
    1 2 3 4 5

13. Does the senior management understand that a successful brand will increase shareholder value?
    1 2 3 4 5

14. Do the various departments throughout the company clearly understand the brand position, platform and objectives?   1 2 3 4 5

CUSTOMER

15. Does your target audience really know your category is available?
    1 2 3 4 5

16. Do you make a conscious effort to make your customers/target audience feel like a friend?
    1 2 3 4 5

17. How well do you know your customer's tastes and thinking?
    1 2 3 4 5

18. Have you asked your customers what they think of your brand in the last 12 months?
    1 2 3 4 5

19. Have you worked at improving your customer's experience when they are going through the purchasing process?
    1 2 3 4 5

PRODUCT

20. Do you honestly see any weaknesses in your products or services?
    1 2 3 4 5

21. Are you continually making product or service improvements?
    1 2 3 4 5

22. Does the quality and price of your brand meet or exceed your customer's expectations?
    1 2 3 4 5

23. Do you know what your brand stands for?
    1 2 3 4 5

24. Are you a "me too" product? Are there many of the same types of products or services in your category?
    1 2 3 4 5

25. Is your product designed to meet or exceed your consumers perception of the category?
    1 2 3 4 5

MARKETING

26. Have you built a complete and real life profile of your perfect target audience, including a day/week in the life of scenarios etc?
    1 2 3 4 5

27. Do you evaluate the effectiveness of last years marketing programs?
    1 2 3 4 5

28. Do you follow the same marketing plans that you created last year?
    1 2 3 4 5

29. Have you identified outside factors (economy, supply of raw materials, weather, labor supply, stock market etc) that could affect your brand?
    1 2 3 4 5

30. Are all of your communication pieces, including logos, brochures, advertising, PR, promotions coordinated to get maximum impact?
    1 2 3 4 5

31. If you have a 2-step distribution product, do you in control of the way your brand is being represented? (If not, give yourself a 3)
    1 2 3 4 5

32. Do you have a set of guidelines for your graphic communications?
    1 2 3 4 5

33. Does the sales department have input into the marketing programs?
    1 2 3 4 5

34. Is your brand image being consistently delivered across all media and communications, including Advertising, promotions, internal & external mail, brochures etc?
    1 2 3 4 5

35. Do you have a position statement, and is it registered?
    1 2 3 4 5

36. Have you asked your customers, "what makes us different"?
    1 2 3 4 5

37. Do you know, if your customers feel your product gives added value to the category they are buying?
    1 2 3 4 5

38. What effect does your customer's value of your brand have in developing your pricing?
    1 2 3 4 5

39. Do you know what your customers like or dislike about your brand?
    1 2 3 4 5

40. Have you truly found out what your customers really want in your brand and done something to meet those needs?
    1 2 3 4 5

41. During market dips are you reluctant to cut back your marketing programs?
    1 2 3 4 5

42. Do you have a short and long-term plan for the brand?
    1 2 3 4 5

43. Do you have a brand commitment statement?
    1 2 3 4 5

44. Is your marketing and branding programs based on research?
    1 2 3 4 5

See next page for details on what your score means!

TOTAL_____

1 - 44   POOR you are in trouble! (call Jack Sims immediately)

45 - 90 AVERAGE try to focus on your brand more!

91 - 135 OK BRAND you are well on your way!

136 - 180 SUPERBRAND you will be a bran leader soon!

181 - 220 AMAZING you can't be this good!

THE TOP 10 WAYS TO IDENTIFY YOUR MOST PROFITABLE TARGETS

Decision-making power: the more responsibility the target has for making a buying decision, the more valuable the target.

Sales potential: the more a target buys within or has used the product category, the more valuable the target.

Growth potential: The more a target group is growing, the more valuable the target group.

Lifetime value: The more a target is expected to buy a product over the target's lifetime, the more valuable the target.

Retention potential: The more likely it is that a target can be economically sustained and, therefore, retained over time, the more valuable the target.

Common motivations: The more homogeneous and likely to be pre-empted the target's needs are, the more valuable the target.

Problem potential: The bigger the problem the target has that the marketer can solve, the more valuable the target.

Responsiveness: The more a target responds to a company's marketing efforts, the more valuable the target.

Media exposure patterns and media costs: The easier and less expensive it is to reach a target with media, the more valuable the target.

Findability: The more easily a target can be identified in databases, the more valuable the target.

COMPANY QUESTIONS

1. Gross Sales/revenue of each customer.

2. Net profit of each Customer.

3. What is the average lifetime of your customer base?

4. What is the lifetime value of a customer? In other words the average profit over the lifetime of the relationship.

5. Customer % of their spending in your category. What is your share of their total category spending?

6. What are the satisfaction ratings that a customer gives to your products, service or relationships?

7. How does management interact with customers?

8. How do your employees interact with customers?

9. What messages are you sending your customer base, and how are you sending them?

10. How do you follow up with your customers?

11. How quickly and frequently are you getting updated information on your customers?

12. What really describes your business?
    A) Customer Centric B) Low cost provider C) Product innovator D) Other

13. What is your "Business to Business" USP (Unique Selling Proposition), are you easy to do business with?

14. What is your unique difference to your competition?

PARTNERS IN BUSINESS QUESTIONS

Rank - Satisfaction 1-10   Importance 1-10   Gap 1-10

How are we doing so far?

How are we on service?

Are we reliable?

Do we get our products to you on time?

How is our product quality?

What needs are we not getting fulfilled?

What is the responsiveness of our employees?

Generally, what is the attitude of our company?

What 3 areas would you like to see us improve, and in what order?

What 3 areas are we best at?

What are our competition's 3 best attributes?

What can we do together to improve your business?

THE HIRING PROCESS
Hiring is a process, not an act!

Things to do when hiring personnel:

The person you hire will determine the results you get on the job! Before you start your candidate search, IDENTIFY YOUR NEEDS. Consider how this person will fit in the bigger picture: company culture, management style, existing employees, what the job specifications are.

CANDIDATE SEARCH

Establish a good working relationship with your recruiter/search firm. This will save you lots of time—a good recruiter should have a solid understanding of more than just the skills you need and what your company does: He/she should know the culture and personality of your firm. Recruiter should be able to identify talent even when there is no open position and bring the candidate to your attention.

INTERVIEWING

GOAL of interviewing is more than just gathering facts: You want a clear picture of past accomplishments and track record, how he/she will handle different situations, how their past experience will transfer over to your company. Define your hiring goals, know what you are looking for in a candidate, and then develop a predetermined list of questions, which should change for different jobs. This will maintain consistency in interviewing all candidates.

LET THE CANDIDATE DO MORE OF THE TALKING!!!!

A common mistake by an employer not used to interviewing is to tell the candidate too much initially about what the job requires and what they are looking for...this allows the candidate to answer with what they think you want to hear. Your job as the interviewer is to listen and evaluate.

DON'T ask many yes/no questions—ask open-ended questions; situational and behavioral questions like:

Tell me about a time when...

How would you handle this situation...

Describe your most significant accomplishment...

Describe the culture/philosophy of your former firms...

Make sure the candidate explains the structure of his past firms and how they fit into the picture—you need to determine if it is applicable to your firm.

CONTROL THE INTERVIEW—your time is valuable. Once you determine a candidate is not suitable, do NOT feel obligated to spend a lot of time with them.

REFERENCES are so important; many employers do not thoroughly check references. References can help determine what the previous employer's methods of measuring performance were and how the company is similar or different from yours. A candidate who was a good fit with one firm may not necessarily be a good fit for yours. It is important through interviewing and reference checking to get a sense of the past employer's organizational structure.

GET AT LEAST 3 PEOPLE IN YOUR ORGANIZATION TO INTERVIEW THE CANDIDATE! The interviewers don't have to be from the department that is going to hire, but a completely different perspective will come from this exercise. It also involves more than one department and shows the current employees that you value their input.

OVERALL, MAKE SURE THAT YOU CONDUCT AN ONGOING SEARCH FOR TALENTED PEOPLE WHO WILL ENHANCE AND GROW YOUR COMPANY. These people are out there; you just have not managed to find them yet.

FINALLY, make sure that you conduct ongoing reviews about your employees; the biggest problem of most companies is that they "hire in haste and fire at leisure." Remember, the people who are usually looking for jobs are in the bottom quartile of the hiring talent pool. So when you suddenly find out that you are going to lose a valuable employee, you will only get applications from the people who are currently looking. And there is usually a reason for that!

CREATIVE BRIEFING FORM

Client..

Job # and Name..

BACKGROUND INFORMATION:
Brand
history_____

_____

Product
positioning_____

Available
research_____

Brand condition and state of the category

_____

_____

Examples of current campaigns available
_____
Samples of other communications that exemplify the required direction_____
What are we creating and
why?_____

_____

How are we going to achieve success?_____

_____

BRAND PERSONALITY/ESSENCE

Brand
values_____

Brand
benefits_____

Brand
credibilty_____

Why consumers buy this
brand?_____
How will the program be implemented?
_____
_____

Who are we talking to, and what RELEVANT customer insights do we have about them?
_____

Describe the response we want.

What's the SINGLE MOST COMPELLING thing you can tell them to elicit this response?

What's the proof?

How will we know if we have succeeded?

Is there anything that could AFFECT the work?

Jack Sims

COMMUNICATION PRIORITIES

Rank in order_____

Copy direction_____

_____

Mood Tone and manner of the creative direction

_____
_____
_____

TECHNICAL INFORMATION
Vehicle_____
Size_____Drop
Date_____
Legal requirements, trade marks, logo's etc._____

_____

Additional information

The timetable for delivery is!
Estimate costs...... Brief creative......... Concept by 1st ....
Layouts by..........Layout to client by....... Pre-production......
Photography begins...............Production starts...............

Delivery date

Creative budget in hours

Additional expected costs.

Signed and approved by

Copyright Jack Sims 2002

CONCLUSION

I do hope that you have managed to get a great deal of information from this book and are able to apply it to your company. Please realize that you cannot do everything in one go, brands are built over time. Your brand is probably one of the most important components of your company and honestly it is an area that most of us do not focus enough on. It really can be the difference between you and your competition If you are passionate about your brand and share that passion with the people you work with, your clients and your suppliers I promise you will be well on your way to becoming a brand leader in your category.

Thanks you for reading this book and I wish you all the best of luck in whatever you do, and to quote John Lennon, "Give peace a chance".

FOR BOOKING KEYNOTES AND SEMINARS
CONTACT JACK AT:

Phone 649 946 4136
e-mail: brandtothbone@earthlink.com
web site: www.jacksims.com

or write:
Jack Sims
PO Box 694800
Miami,
Florida 33269

NOTES:

NOTES: